ONE GALLANT RUSH

ONE GALLANT RUSH

*Robert Gould Shaw
and His Brave Black Regiment*

by Peter Burchard

St. Martin's Press · New York

TO GUY DEMING

Right in the van,
On the red rampart's slippery swell,
    With heart that beat a charge, he fell
    Foeward, as fits a man;
But the high soul burns on to light men's feet
Where death for noble ends makes dying sweet.

JAMES RUSSELL LOWELL, 1863
Memoriæ Positum   R. G. Shaw

He is out of bounds now. He rejoices in man's lovely,
peculiar power to choose life and die —
when he leads his black soldiers to death,
he cannot bend his back.

ROBERT LOWELL, 1964
For The Union Dead

Note for Paperback Edition

When I wrote this book, Americans of African descent were called Negroes. Since then, they have been designated as blacks, Afro-Americans, and African-Americans. There is widespread disagreement among Americans of African descent as to what they should in fact be called. As you read, please bear in mind that terms used in quotes were current in the nineteenth century and that this book was first published in 1965, when the use of the word Negro, with a capital, was common and preferred.

—Peter Burchard
Williamstown, Massachusetts
May 1989

FOREWORD

This is the story of Robert Gould Shaw and the Fifty-Fourth Massachusetts Regiment, the first Negro fighting unit raised in the North in the Civil War.

Robert Gould Shaw's feeling about his work coincided with that of one of his officers, William H. Simkins, who wrote of his decision to serve under Shaw, "This is no hasty conclusion, no blind leap of an enthusiast, but the result of much hard thinking. It will not be at first, and probably not for a long time, an agreeable position, for many reasons too evident to state. . . . Then this is nothing but an experiment after all; but it is an experiment that I think it high time we should try,—an experiment which, the sooner we prove fortunate the sooner we can count upon an immense number of hardy troops . . . an experiment which the sooner we prove unsuccessful, the sooner we shall establish an important truth and rid ourselves of a false hope."

When, early in 1863, Governor John Albion Andrew of Massachusetts was given permission by Secretary of War Stanton to raise a regiment of free Negroes, the leaders of the antislavery crusade thought of the project as a tangible result of their life's work. They gave the regiment resounding support. When Shaw, his officers and men marched through Boston on their way to war, the tough and implacable William Lloyd Garrison stood on Wendell Phillips's balcony on Essex Street weeping for joy as the Negroes of the Fifty-Fourth pasesd by.

Young Robert Gould Shaw, a product of educated antislavery society, was for five critical months in command of the Fifty-Fourth. He took a fine body of men from his own country and Canada and shaped them into a proud regiment, led them to war and died in the vanguard of a great charge against the gates of Charleston.

Other Negro regiments had come into being before Andrew presented the Fifty-Fourth's colors to Shaw. But these had been sanctioned only grudgingly, raised in a raggle-taggle fashion and had consisted mostly of escaped or abandoned slaves. Negroes had performed well in skirmishes, and at Port Hudson in Louisiana a force of 1,080 blacks under Colonel John A. Nelson had three times charged a fort protected in front by a deep and almost impassable bayou. The attack had moved General Banks to report that "their conduct was heroic; no troops could be more determined or daring. . . ."

But it remained for Shaw, his carefully chosen officers and men, to write a story of Negro bravery for all the world to see, to pave the way for widespread participation of the American Negro in what, with the signing of the Emancipation Proclamation, had become his own crusade.

Thomas Wentworth Higginson, who himself commanded a regiment of Negroes and whose *Army Life in a Black Regiment* has become a minor American classic, wrote for *Century Magazine* in 1897, "The attack on Fort Wagner, with the picturesque and gallant death of young Colonel Shaw, made a great impression on the North, and did more than anything else, perhaps, to convince the public that Negro troops could fight well, not merely as skirmishers, but in line of battle."

As Shaw's men waited in the twilight for the signal to storm Fort Wagner, some of them might well have thought of Negro leader Frederick Douglass's words, "The iron gate of our prison stands half open, one gallant rush . . . will fling it wide."

PETER BURCHARD
New York, N.Y.
January 1965

CONTENTS

ACKNOWLEDGMENTS

I am especially indebted to John Anthony Scott without whose encouragement and generous help this book would have been far less complete and, in fact, might not have seen the light of day at all. Thanks, too, to Ormonde de Kay for his assistance in gathering material.

Without the facilities of the Frederick Lewis Allen Memorial Room at the Main Branch of the New York Public Library, the time required to write this book would have been tripled. My thanks to Gilbert A. Cam for putting the privileges of the Allen Room at my disposal. I owe a debt to many people on the staff of the New York Public Library, among them Barbara Gibson for prompt delivery of books to the Allen Room. In the American History Division, Sherry L. Spranger, Fred Wellerford and Leon Weidman were particularly helpful. The Rare Book Division's Lewis Stark, Maud Cole, Barry Minkin and Philomena Houlihan deserve a vote of thanks. Thanks too, to the Map Division staff.

Thanks to Mike Petro in the Microfilm Department at the New York *Herald Tribune*, and to the staff of the Staten Island Historical Society.

My researches in Boston were particularly pleasant. John Alden, Keeper of Rare Books at the Boston Public Library, pointed the way to other material in other libraries and his staff was most helpful. Thanks, too, to the staffs at The Houghton Library, Harvard University, the Massachusetts Historical Society and the Boston Athenæum.

I would like to thank John Farrar of Farrar, Straus and Giroux for permission to use a verse of Robert Lowell's "For the Union Dead" from *For the Union Dead* by Robert Lowell published in 1964.

My thanks to Lester Inabinett, Director of the South Caroliniana Library, The University of South Carolina, for his letter about the trial of the Negro prisoners at Charleston and a transcript of the letter from the Milledge Luke Bonham Papers.

ONE GALLANT RUSH

1.

May 28 was a brilliant day in the city of Boston. On Beacon Street, the rose-colored brick of the houses warmed in the sun. Morning sunlight touched the leaves of the trees in the Public Garden and on the Common and glistened on the Charles River.

The sounds of music and marching and clattering hooves were heard in the streets of the city where Crispus Attucks had shed his blood and where in 1835 William Lloyd Garrison had crossed the ground where Attucks had died—Garrison led like a barnyard animal by a rope, taunted by a mob and barely escaping with his life. The city police were out in force, their buttons gleaming, their gloves spotless.

Now the crowds lining Beacon Street saw columns of soldiers moving down the hill. As the music came louder and the thump and rattle of the drums grew more distinct, the dark faces of the men in the ranks were seen clearly, eyes front. At the head of his regiment, with Patrick Gilmore's marching band, rode Robert Gould Shaw, the young colonel of the regiment, his back straight, his bright sword held in his gloved right hand, the muscles of his horse's flanks reflecting the sky like polished silver. Shaw's skin was pale above the faces of his men. His white officers were some of the best battle-tempered youths of the day, and marching beside them were the finest of Negroes—men who had drilled through the winter and who marched proudly, holding their rifles in their strong brown hands.

Members of Shaw's family were gathered behind the lacy iron-work of a second-floor balcony at 44 Beacon Street. The house, which belonged to Shaw's mother's family, was much like the other houses facing the Common. The graceful arched doorway was framed by a shallow portico supported by two Corinthian columns, and three marble steps led up from the brick sidewalk.

As Shaw drew abreast of the doorway, he raised his sword and kissed it, turning his head to glance for a moment at the familiar faces above the crowd. Then he lowered the sword and rode on down the hill.

In Civil War days, state governors raised regiments for Federal service. The regiment marching through Boston this day had been sponsored by John Albion Andrew, the popular wartime governor of Massachusetts. Andrew had long favored the enlistment of Negroes in regiments raised for Federal service. After the issuance of the Emancipation Proclamation, believing that American Negroes at last had something to fight for, he had gone to Stanton and obtained the order under which the Fifty-Fourth Massachusetts was organized:

War Department
Washington City, Jan. 26, 1863

Ordered: That Governor Andrew of Massachusetts is authorized, until further orders, to raise such numbers of volunteers, companies of artillery for duty in the forts of Massachusetts and elsewhere, and such corps of infantry for the volunteer military service as he may find convenient, such volunteers to be enlisted for three years, or until sooner discharged, and may include persons of African descent, organized into special corps. He will make the usual needful requisitions on the appropriate staff bureaus and officers, for the proper transportation, organization, supplies, subsistence, arms and equipments of such volunteers.

EDWIN M. STANTON,
Secretary of War.

With the order in his pocket, Andrew hurried back to Boston to begin recruiting before Stanton might have a chance to reconsider.

On February 2, a letter from Andrew was delivered to Robert Gould Shaw's father, Francis George Shaw, at his home in West New Brighton on Staten Island. Andrew was an old friend of Francis Shaw. He had written that he considered that this would be the most important corps to be organized since the start of the war. Andrew believed firmly that freedom would be of little value to the American Negro if he did not fight for it himself. He had written that he wished to offer the colonelcy of the new regiment to Robert Gould Shaw.

Andrew was anxious that the officers be young men of exceptional character and firm antislavery principles. He wanted them to be above a "vulgar contempt for color."

At the time his father received Andrew's letter, Robert Gould

Shaw was twenty-five years old. He was serving as a captain in the
Second Massachusetts Regiment in camp near Stafford Courthouse
in Virginia. Captain Shaw, already battle-hardened, was a handsome young man, intelligent and sensitive, and a soldier of unques-
tioned bravery. He was short and erect in his bearing, had blond hair
and delicate, well-cut features. He was described as having a charming, easy manner and a lively disposition. In an age when sentimen-
tality was rife, he revealed little sentiment in his letters or his speech.

Shaw's father immediately acknowledged receipt of the Governor's
letter and said he felt the matter so important that he would leave
that night to convey to his son the Governor's offer.

2.

Robert Gould Shaw was born in Boston on October 10, 1837, into a world of gentility and wealth and what must have been a life of considerable ease. He was a second child, the first being a girl named Anne. His mother, Sarah Blake Sturgis, was the daughter of a distinguished merchant. Shaw's great-greatuncle, Major Samuel Shaw, had fought with distinction in the American Revolution, had served briefly as a secretary in the Department of War, had been first Consul of the United States at Canton and had engaged in tremendously profitable trade with China. Through investment in the growing commerce of the country—foreign trade, railroads, manufacturing and real estate—Shaw dollars had multiplied. In the best tradition of nineteenth-century New England, the Shaws took their social obligations seriously, and by the time Robert Gould Shaw was born his parents had developed an interest in the blossoming antislavery crusade.

When Rob was five, his father bought a large estate in West Roxbury adjacent to Brook Farm, site of the experiment in utopian living. Brook Farmers hoped to provide for themselves a more simple, wholesome way of life than could be found in the outside world. Shaw's father contributed to the support of the farm and the Shaws, who were intimates of George Ripley, founder and helmsman of the project, spent much of their time there in the midst of that perpetual round of physical, artistic and intellectual activity. The place was nine miles from the center of Boston. Oglers from the city and the surrounding countryside were called "civilisees."

Brook Farmers were a brilliant company, many of them literary or clerical figures of the day. Nathaniel Hawthorne lived at the farm and Emerson was a frequent visitor though not an active participator. Ripley, a great cheerful man who had for fourteen years been a Unitarian preacher, was a monumental doer of farm chores. He milked cows, cleaned stalls and directed work in the fields. He gave lectures in philosophy, astronomy and mathematics. Charles A. Dana taught Greek and German, and John Sullivan Dwight—a wispy, happy little man, later to become the leader of the Boston music world—gave music lessons.

Most members of the Brook Farm community were highly individualistic. They subscribed to no creed and took instruction in a given art or science only if they were strongly drawn to it. Life at the farm was not all work. There were dances and picnics, there was boating on the Charles and a drive to Boston now and then to attend concerts and antislavery meetings at Faneuil Hall.

While in West Roxbury, Shaw attended the primary school of Miss Mary Peabody, sister of the more prominent Elizabeth, in her later years called "the Grandmother of Boston" and painted as Miss Birdseye in the razor-edged satirical prose of Henry James.

Shaw bore his grandfather's name. The old man, just before he died, summoned Shaw and another grandson, Henry S. Russell,[1] to his bedside. Old Robert Gould Shaw looked hard at the two boys and said, "My children, I am leaving the stage of action and you are entering upon it. I exhort you to use your example and influence against intemperance and slavery."

Rob's father had no need to work to support his family and worked instead for the public good. His and his wife's participation in the antislavery crusade became more intense as the years went by. The Shaws numbered among their friends such luminaries of the movement as William Lloyd Garrison, John A. Andrew, Charles Sumner, Theodore Parker, Edmund Quincy, Lydia Maria Child, Wendell Phillips, the much admired British-born actress Frances Anne Kemble and a host of others.

Journalist and author Sidney Howard Gay,[2] after he had taken up the cause and joined the ranks of this New England intellectual

---

[1] Shaw's cousin, Henry Sturgis Russell, would be a close friend of Shaw through childhood and youth and would serve with him during the war. According to the Harvard Class Book (Report of the Class of 1860—for the years 1900 to 1905), between Shaw and his cousin Harry Russell "there had existed since childhood a close, even romantic friendship."

[2] Sidney Howard Gay, a friend of Francis George Shaw and his family, would join the staff of the powerful *New York Daily Tribune* in 1857, would become its managing editor in 1862. During his term at the *Tribune* and for years thereafter, Gay was a neighbor of the Shaws in West New Brighton on Staten Island.

avant-garde, found the members "to the outside world a set of pesti-
lent fanatics . . . among themselves the most charming circle of
cultivated men and women that it has ever been my lot to know."

In 1846, when Shaw was nine, his family moved to Staten Island
so that his mother could be under the care of Dr. Samuel McKenzie
Elliot, an eminent Scottish doctor who lived and practiced there.
Shaw's mother had an eye ailment and suffered frequent attacks of
rheumatism and neuralgia. But, in spite of bad health, she bore
three more daughters while Shaw was growing up. In his early
years, Rob's attachment to his mother was strong and she exerted
a powerful influence over his thinking. Her surviving letters reveal
her as a pessimistic person, somewhat neurotic and preoccupied with
her health. She had little of her son's brightness of nature or
sense of humor. Her singleness of devotion to the antislavery cause
prompted one of Shaw's fellow officers in the Fifty-Fourth to describe
her as having "rare and high traits of mind and heart . . ." and she
inspired loyalty and confidence in her friends. In their letters to her,
Maria Lowell,[3] Fanny Kemble, Lydia Maria Child and others revealed their deepest feelings. Mrs. Shaw was something of a doting
mother. But despite the strength of her character, Shaw developed
a mind of his own.

Staten Island was mostly rural when the Shaws moved there.
There were settlements of seagoing men and stevedores close to the
docks, but much of the land was farmed. On the island, there were
large estates belonging to Winants, Camerons and Van Pelts. Mrs.
Shaw's doctor owned a large tract of land and a number of houses
overlooking Kill Van Kull which ran hard by the northern extremity
of the island. The Shaws settled in the doctor's neighborhood. Off
to the east, Robbins Reef Lighthouse flashed its signal in the night,
and, beyond the light stretched the broad expanse of New York
Harbor—a delight to the eye on a clear day.

Shaw was sent to a small private school on Staten Island and a
year later, though his parents were Unitarians, to St. John's College
Roman Catholic School at Fordham.

He wrote from Fordham, "I got here safe and sound, and haven't
felt hungry yet though it is not far from supper time. I wish you
hadn't sent me here while you are on the island, because I want

---

[3] Maria (White) Lowell was the wife of the poet James Russell Lowell.
She died in 1853.

to be there, and now I have to stay at this old place. I'm sure I shan't want to come here after vacation for I hate it like everything. . . . I always feel ugly when I think of home."

Shaw was an imaginative boy. He delighted in the stories of Washington Irving, which he found enormously funny. He loved music and had a gift for drawing. While at Fordham, he sketched from the pictures of other artists, drew pictures from his "own mind" and illustrated stories he had read. He sent his mother his illustrations. "I drew these pictures last night: that one where the Berber is going fast is where he stole the Emperor's boy and they are chasing him. . . ."

In September he ran away from school to rejoin his family but his father took him straight back. This first desertion was treated sternly but the ferule was spared.

A week or so later, Shaw wrote, "If they had whipped me then I am almost certain I should have run away again, I should have been so mad. As it was I came near going the second time I was sent out of the study room. One of the boys ran away from here during vacation, and they thought he was up here; but he went aboard a sloop on the Hudson river and worked there for a month.

"After I came up from New York with Father, this boy asked me to run away with him again, and do the same as he did before; and I would have done it then if it wasn't getting cold, but I wouldn't do it now. I felt sort of angry then, because I had to come back; and if I got punished when I didn't do anything, I should feel just like going off, and don't know but what I would if I got a good chance."

Rob's mother, worried by this streak of rebellion, asked him to write her every week and, in a petulant tone, he reasserted his independence. "I don't want to write every week, it's too much trouble, and I shall only write when I want something. If you think I'm sick when I don't write, you can send for me to come and tell you. . . ."

Rob was desperately homesick all that fall. "Whenever I think of home it makes me feel like crying, and sometimes I can't help crying before all the boys."

Of a teacher he wrote, "My old teacher scolded me today because I didn't do something he didn't tell me to do, and I hate him like everything. He is the worst old fellow I ever saw." His intense distaste for the life at Fordham was something Shaw never quite forgot, and his violent reaction to what he thought was injustice became a signal trait in his later years. He was easily led but could not be driven.

Rob was released from bondage in January of 1851 when, to his intense delight, his parents took him out of school so they could sail to Europe *en famille*.

3.

Rob spent a summer in Switzerland with his parents and sisters and in the fall, while his family traveled, went to the school of M. Roulet in Neuchâtel. He loved Neuchâtel and rhapsodized about the school.

The window of his room faced the mountains and on clear days he could see Mont Blanc, the Jungfrau and lesser peaks burning white against the sky. He suffered from touches of loneliness once in awhile and wrote his mother, "I keep thinking of what you are doing all the time, and when I thought you were on the journey I kept thinking to myself how you and Father were sitting in the coupe in front, and the children playing inside, the same as we did before, and when the time came we usually stopped to get dinner or bait the horses. . . ."

M. Roulet was a just master and got "mad" only when the boys broke the rules or were impolite. "But when he does get angry he's just like a wolf and calls the boys all kinds of names." M. Roulet thought it "wonderfully strange" that Rob should want his window open while he slept but let it stay open until ten o'clock.

Shaw's mother, herself an assertive person, urged Shaw to declare his faith to his Catholic schoolmates in ringing terms but Shaw rejected her appeal. "You said something about not being afraid of declaring one's opinions. I'm sure I wouldn't be afraid of saying we were Unitarians if there could be any kind of use in it, but, as it is, it would bring up discussion and conversations which would be very tiresome, and as I don't want to become a reformer, apostle, or anything of that kind, there is no use doing disagreeable things for nothing."

During his two years in Neuchâtel, Shaw and M. Roulet became fast friends, and though he never had an appetite for scholarly pursuits, Shaw developed into a thoughtful young man. He read novels and plays in English and French, played the violin and walked with his schoolmates in Swiss mountain trails. He read Byron's poems,

which filled him with a desire "to make some too." But poetry was
not his forte. He seldom got further than a first line.

During the summer of 1853, Shaw and his schoolmates went
with M. Roulet on trips to the mountains, lakes and forests of
Switzerland. Then, late in August, Shaw traveled to Sorrento, where
his family was spending a few weeks by the sea.

Fanny Kemble was spending the summer in Sorrento and renewed
her friendship with the Shaws. The actress, firm in her antislavery
views, though never thinking of herself as an Abolitionist, had lived
fifteen years previously with her husband Pierce Butler on the largest
plantation in the state of Georgia. Her marriage to Butler had been
dissolved and in later years she would write of it as a "disastrous
and lamentable relation."

Fanny Kemble wrote of Italian palaces in Sorrento, "built of
marble, and rising out of orange groves, and commanding from
every window, terrace and balcony, incomparable views of seas,
shores, and islands, renowned in history and poetry and lovelier than
imagination. . . .

"Our windows sweep the whole bay, from Capo di Monte to the
little toe of Naples."

This remarkable woman was described by the Swedish novelist
Fredrika Bremer in these terms: "Her countenance fine without
being beautiful, and rich and magnificent in expression. . . ." Maria
Lowell had said of her, "In her smiles there are fifty smiles." Fanny
Kemble told the Shaws stories of her plantation days. She had developed deep concern for her husband's slaves, tending the sick and
defending the Negroes against injustice.

After publication of her *Journal of a Residence on a Georgia Plantation*, Lydia Maria Child would write of Fanny Kemble, whom she
had never much liked, "while reading her journal, my soul was con-
strained to do her homage. To look right through the shams of
slavery as she did, indicates a clearness of moral perception belonging only to honest and truthful natures. And for a petted celebrity,
as she was accustomed to elegance and refinement, to minister so
kindly and conscientiously to those poor and loathsome slaves, proves
a rare nobility of soul."

Most of Butler's slaves thought of him as a just master. But his
overseers were not always so humane, and Fanny Kemble had often
found herself "in a perfect agony of distress for the slaves."

In her diary of 1838–1839 she had recorded an episode in her life on Butler's plantation:

> This morning I paid my second visit to the infirmary, and found there had been some faint attempt at sweeping and cleaning, in compliance with my entreaties. The poor woman Harriet, however, whose statement with regard to the impossibility of their attending properly to their children had been so vehemently denied by the overseer, was crying bitterly. I asked her what ailed her, when, more by signs and dumb show than words, she and old Rose informed me that Mr. O—— had flogged her that morning for having told me that the woman had not time to keep their children clean. It is part of the regular duty of the overseer to visit the Infirmary at least once a day, which he generally does in the morning, and Mr. O——'s visit had preceeded mine but a short time only, or I would have been edified by seeing a man horsewhip a woman.

Fanny Kemble's stories of first-hand experiences with the institution which Shaw instinctively rejected and had been taught to despise, her passionate rejection of its injustices and inhumanities, made a deep impression on his youthful mind.

Shaw studied in Italy for a year and, in 1854, at sixteen, he left his family to study in Hanover. He was charmed by the ancient town on the Leine with its narrow streets and gingerbread houses, its market square, handsome theater and opera house. His rooms were spacious and pleasant and he enjoyed more freedom than he had ever known before. In the evenings he dined about the city with friends and went to the opera at least once a week.

In August of 1854, he wrote his mother, "You can't conceive how big inside I've got since I've been here. I'm at least five years older than when I came; but it is a natural consequence of being left alone and at my own disposition. I begin to find you treat me too little in your letters."

In February he saw A Midsummer Night's Dream for the second time. "The muscles of my stomach are a little sore this morning. . . . Last night when Thisbe killed herself, she made a great many funny faces, and everybody laughed very much; and after she had lain down (it's a man you know), I saw her shaking all over, from top to toe with laughter, and when she got up, her face was very red with laughing. It was fun to see all the other actors trying to hold in."

While in Hanover, the slim, elegant youth went to dinners and balls and was much admired by German girls. But at seventeen he took girls lightly. He went to one costume ball dressed as a "lady," having shaved off his downy, blond beard so the masquerade would be complete. His friends were fooled until he spoke in a "swaggering voice" which astonished them all. At more than one party, forgetting his grandfather's exhortation to avoid intemperance, he made merry all night, drinking more than his share of German wine.

Shaw kept up a lively interest in events at home. As was natural because of his background and his recent visits with Fanny Kemble, he took special note of antislavery news and stories about American Negroes. He was a regular reader of the *New York Daily Tribune*, which not only reported local news and news of the battles of the Crimean War but printed the complete texts of Henry Ward Beecher's antislavery sermons, stories of the horrors of slave auctions in New Orleans and a liberal scattering of items like these:

Feb. 19, 1855
MULATTO BOY TURNED OUT OF SCHOOL—A few days since, Miss Isabella Newhall, a teacher in one of the public schools in Cincinnati, applied to the board of education of that city, soliciting the dismission of one of her pupils, not for improper conduct, nor on account of his inability or unwillingness to receive instruction, but because his skin was darker than that of some of the other scholars. . . .

The pupil in question was in fact dismissed by a vote of the school board (fifteen to ten) and two board members resigned.

Feb. 21, 1855
SLAVERY NATIONALIZED—Washington, Saturday, Feb. 17, 1855. Ten righteous men in the Senate! A bill passed the Senate yesterday to pay (out of the National Treasury) to certain Indians full compensation for the loss of a number of slaves—thus recognizing "the wild and guilty fantasy" of property in human flesh. Who says now that Slavery is not national?

The ten righteous men were of course the Dissenters.

Then, again on a more personal level, the *Tribune* reported an injustice in New York City.

Feb. 27, 1855
NEW YORK SCENE—A little before 9 o'clock on a Saturday evening, a decent looking colored woman entered one of the Eighth -av. cars

on Canal st. and had reached the middle of it when the conductor observed her and ordered her to go out, which she refused to do, telling him that she wished to ride and had a *right* to do so, as had recently been established by a judicial decision in Brooklyn. The conductor replied that his orders were imperative (referring to orders from his employers), and again ordered her out. She still refused to go, when he clinched her, and, with the aid of the driver, after a desperate struggle of some minutes, forced her into the middle of the street, where she was left in the bitter cold, her clothes badly torn and herself somewhat injured. . .

Hanover was fine that spring. Shaw, who had developed into quite a linguist, took Spanish lessons and read the works of Goethe and Schiller in German. On warm evenings he dallied with his friends in the public gardens where the students took their coffee and listened to the music of military bands. "Sometimes there are two or even three bands together and the music is often splendid. . . ."

Shaw expressed irritation at prejudice against America in the German press. He complained that German journalists picked up and magnified his country's faults and printed little about her virtues. But he developed an affection for Germans of his acquaintance. He wrote with dry humor of one of the town's more colorful characters:

"The gentleman here who had not drank any water for twenty years made a pretty great sensation among all his acquaintances by drinking a glass of water the other night at a party. He is a great, fat fellow, and whenever I go to his house he runs me down for being so thin. He told me yesterday that if I didn't begin and drink two bottles of Rhine wine every day at dinner I should run to seed, and that if I did I should be fat as butter at the end of a year. He says it's the only thing that saved him from consumption. . . . He drinks a bottle of wine or beer at supper and at breakfast and I don't know how many at dinner. He's going to make a journey to the Rhine soon, because he feels the consumption coming on again; and he says when he's there he'll do nothing but drink and sleep in the grass. If I followed the advice he drives into me every time I see him I should be done for in less than no time."

Shaw liked the man in spite of his dissolute character but liked his daughter even better. The girl, just fourteen when Shaw knew her, promised to be a great beauty. Even after he left Hanover, Shaw found it hard to get her out of his mind.

Late in June, Shaw read of a slave being taken from jail and burned alive in Alabama. The account, which had first been published in a Mississippi paper, was reprinted in the *Tribune*. The story was graphic, telling of the Negro's attempted rape and eventual murder of a white girl. The man, tied to a willow stake and standing on a pile of dry wood, had confessed his guilt in a shaking voice. He had killed the girl in the fear that she would tell of his molestation, though she had protested that she never would tell.

A huge crowd of people, slaves and whites, witnessed the ghastly execution, carried out at the scene of the crime. The victim's "fearful cries resounded through the air, while the surrounding Negroes who witnessed his dreadful agony and horrible contortions sent up an involuntary howl of horror."

As the man died, "his black and burning carcass, like a demon of fire, grinned as if in hellish triumph at his tormentors."

The event was described by a reporter for the *Marion Mississippi Republican* as having had a "salutary effect upon the two thousand slaves who witnessed his execution . . . a thousand deaths of the kind are too good for a devil like negro Dave."

The story made a vivid impression on Shaw. He wrote of the burning, "I didn't think the last would ever happen again."

In August, Shaw sailed from Kiel to Norway with a couple of his student friends, one of them a young man he called Heinrich, for whom he later expressed affection in his letters. The crossing was fine, the sunsets spectacular. At Christiania, they bought two gigs and traveled around the countryside, living mostly on oatmeal bread and milk and sleeping in the huts and barns of country folk. By posting, a system of swapping horses at various stops, they traveled fast, in short stages, never using a horse more than two hours.

Shaw was impressed by the stark beauty of the landscape and the slight difference between night and day. He liked the Norwegians and soon learned to understand Danish, which was common in Norway at that time. With his friends, he spent a couple of days in a Laplander's hut. He was fascinated by the rugged herdsmen and the primitive conditions in which they lived. He wrote, "The family with whom we stayed had 600 reindeer."

Shaw's family had returned to America in June. Shaw wrote them at Newport. "What awful riots there have been in America lately. I don't know how the Country seems to those who are living in it, but looking at it through American as well as German newspapers it seems pretty ill and sick."

Life in mid-nineteenth-century Hanover was noisy and gay. Shaw went to a *polterabend,* a prenuptial evening party. "When the people are sitting at supper the servants from the neighboring houses come and throw jars, bottles, tumblers, and anything made of glass against the door of the house, or on the pavement in the courtyard, and make enough noise to deafen a cannoneer; and all this is meant to wish good luck and happiness to 'Braut' and 'Brautigan,' as they are always called. . . ."

Now and then the police made faint attempts to stop these *polterabends* because sometimes the missiles were thrown with so much force that they broke down the doors of the happy houses.

Christmas vacation that year Shaw went to Paris, where he stayed at the Hotel de la Terrasse and walked like a boulevardier along the bustling Champ Élysées. The following week he went to Berlin to spend a few days in the galleries. In January, he wrote his family, "The first of April I shall leave Hanover, and shall arrive in America about the first of May and shall be very glad indeed to go to Cambridge. . . ."

4.

Cambridge was a pleasant place in the 1850's as indeed it is now. The Common in August was brown and dusty, but the clear air, bright sky and the fine warmth of the white-trimmed buildings with glimpses of the Charles River through the trees, should have pleased Shaw. But fresh from two months of study under Francis Barlow[1] on Staten Island and not long away from his frolics in Europe, Shaw saw Harvard as a stylish jail. He passed his entrance examinations with ease but, almost at once, he balked at restrictions. He complained that Harvard was "just like a school."

The first great event of his freshman year was a series of football games with members of the sophomore class. The games, by tradition, were a great melee, a combination of general hazing and open warfare. The class of '60, which would be known as the "fighting class," was larger and made up of bigger boys than any that had come before, so, in the fall of '56, the warfare was especially bloody. The freshmen came out to the fray in straw hats and all their finery and were set upon and beaten roundly in the first two games. In the third game, tradition was shattered. The freshmen triumphed. There were fifty to seventy men on a side and, as the games started, the sophomores came down on the freshmen in a body, knocking down as many as they could. Shaw wrote, "After the first game, few had their own hats on, few a whole shirt, and there were more black eyes, bloody noses and broken teeth than you could well count." Shaw was smaller than most of his classmates and, after the first game, kept sensibly out of the middle of the fray. "My experience in the middle was this: Before I had been there more than a second I had got three fearful raps on the head, was knocked down, and they ran all over me after the ball which had been kicked to an-

---

[1] Francis Barlow was Shaw's tutor on several occasions. Barlow became a brigadier general following the battle of Antietam. He eventually married Shaw's sister, Ellen.

other part of the field. Then I picked myself up . . . and looked
about for my hat among twenty other hats and a good many rags.
I found it a good while afterwards serving as a football to a sophomore during the entr'acte.

"That was Monday and today is Friday, but my head has not got
entirely well yet. I got a good many blows which I didn't feel at all
till the next day. A good many of our fellows were more badly
treated because they had pluck enough to go into the thick of it
each time. Once was enough for me." Shaw wrote glowingly of
freshman Caspar Crowinshield. Crowinshield was a big fellow and
was the undisputed freshman star. "He knocked a fellow from New
York, named Cutting, flat on his back and next day Cutting said
to him mildly, 'You hit me a pretty hard crack last night. . . .'"

As fall wore on, Shaw grew more resigned to the restrictions of
college life and savored its pleasures. He joined a boat club, belonged to the Pierian Sodality, a musical society, and played with
its members in string ensembles. After meetings, the musicians
treated themselves to a round of crackers, cheese and ale. For his
initiation into the society of the Anonyma, Shaw went with the
members to Fresh Pond. "I sang a song and gave a toast, and made
a few appropriate remarks; so you see I am going into public life."

Lacking a zeal for study and with the memory of life in Hanover
still bright, Shaw suffered from occasional fits of despondency. Yet
on the whole he was content. He took an interest in politics and,
like William Lloyd Garrison, believed that the South and its insti-
tutions should be amputated from the Union. Shaw's mother wrote
him at Cambridge, "You may live to see truth and justice prevail
in the Land but I never shall."

Shaw answered, "I can't help hoping there will be disunion some
time, and I suppose there will be before many years. I have been
looking over a good many books lately about America, and almost
all say that slavery is the only fault in America, and we get as much
blame for it as the Southerners, and besides, the disgrace of all their
shameful actions. . . ."

James Russell Lowell had recently returned from Europe to take
up his duties as Professor of Modern Languages at Harvard. Shaw
paid him a visit. "I was surprised to see Mr. Gay last night at Mr.
Lowell's. It was lucky that I happened to go there that night. Mr.

Quincy[2] was there too. He said he thought there would be an immense Republican majority in the next election, and he didn't believe in the Democrats changing their policy, as some may think they will. . . ."

Shaw walked with his classmates in the byways of Cambridge and went to skating parties at Fresh Pond. In spite of the college's restrictions, he found that the boys' rooms were often the scenes of gambling and drinking parties. Shaw did his share of partying as he had in Europe, but he was never especially wild. He got away from Cambridge now and then, crossing the Charles in a horse-drawn omnibus or traveling to New York by the chugging, spark-spreading "Empire State" or one of the night boats that ghosted along Long Island and New England shores, the water reflecting its yellow lights. On the boat trip to New York, Shaw stood at the rail, bundled in woolens, to catch a glimpse of Boston Light or, on the trip back, to watch for the first sight of the beaches and dunes and wintry hills of Scituate and Cohasset.

Shaw found Boston young ladies tiresome. He remembered the German girls. Referring to the daughter of his fat and dissolute Hanoverian friend, he wrote his mother, "I had a letter from Hanover the other day, giving an account of my Love. She has increased in loveliness, sweetness, etc., and especially in playing, so that I entertain thoughts of writing to bespeak her. . . ."

Beyond his belief in a benevolent God, Shaw had no fervent religious convictions. In 1863 he would write, "Since I have been old enough to think for myself, I have considered I had better not try to decide about sects. I always like to hear a good sermon, whether it is preached in an Episcopal or Methodist church. The only Sunday school I ever went to was Episcopal . . ." During his college years Shaw quite often attended the services of Unitarian Theodore Parker. Parker, whose parish was in West Roxbury, was a distinguished scholar. At Faneuil Hall, from his pulpit and elsewhere, Parker had, for many years, delivered himself of abolitionist sentiments. Guest speakers of his persuasion preached from his lectern when he was absent. At Parker's parish in March, Shaw heard, for

---

[2] This was probably Edmund Quincy (1808 to 1877), son of old Josiah Quincy who died in 1864. It might have been Josiah himself. It was probably not Josiah P. Quincy (1829 to 1910). This Quincy, Edmund's nephew, was an unworldly man and wouldn't have been likely to make political predictions.

the first time, a sermon by Wendell Phillips and liked him very much.

As the hard bite of winter relaxed its grip on Massachusetts, the ice in the Charles broke up and the patches of snow on the river's north bank began to disappear. Shaw worked with his fellows in the boating club to take the *Sabrina* out of her wraps and fit her out for the muscle-hardening sport of men. In April, the *Sabrina's* crew, proud as cocks in their boating dress—blue shirts with red facings, straw hats with blue ribbons stamped in gold with the name of their boat—rowed down the Charles. As they moved under bridges, the occupants of carriages, buggies and omnibuses waved at them. They passed under railroad bridges, black against the clear spring sky, and into the harbor to the Navy Yard. "While we were walking there a soldier stepped up and said, 'Are you from the Merrimac,[3] gentlemen?' The Merrimac is a steam frigate lying in the harbor. This question made us feel about three degrees bigger which wasn't small."

Shaw's sister Susie, next born after Shaw,[4] went to school in Cambridge while he was in college there. Shaw visited her often. "I went to meet Susie this morning when she came out of school at recess, and we took a walk together. She seems to like her school and schoolmates very much."

Shaw never wrote for the hand of his young German love, and time and distance dimmed his ardor at last. He wrote to his mother of an unnamed love in New York. "I meant what I said of M.L. (Much Loved), that I was more smitten than before." Then, with a fickleness natural in someone his age, "somehow, though, after I have been away a week I get over it. . . . I had a fine time down there though, and I hope they will ask me again."

In what was then referred to as the "grand financial crash" of

---

[3] The *Merrimac* was destined for fame. In Norfolk Navy Yard at the start of the war, she was scuttled by the Federals, raised by the Confederates and clad in iron sheathing. Rechristened *Virginia*, on her first day in action she destroyed two of the Federal navy's wooden warships. On her second day in action, she was met by the *Monitor* and there followed a colorful, unresolved battle. The *Merrimac* remained afloat for a couple of months, keeping Federal vessels out of the James.

[4] The name of the first-born was Anna. Then came Robert, then Susanna (Susie). After Susie came Josephine (Effie) and Ellen (Nellie) respectively. In December of '57, daughter Anna, now Mrs. George W. Curtis, bore her parents' first grandchild, a boy.

the fall of 1857, some of Shaw's relatives came off badly, but the Shaws themselves, though a little shaken, survived the debacle without a noticeable reduction of income. Shaw wrote his mother from Keene, New Hampshire, where he spent a weekend dancing, skating by moonlight and talking late around a crackling fire. He gave her news of his uncle James Sturgis, all but wiped out in the crash. "Sue and I went out to see Uncle Jim on Tuesday and found him in a very pleasant and comfortable house at Roxbury. He seems in the best of possible spirits and says that he doesn't really care for the loss of money but he is mortified at being of no account in State Street, after being so much there. He creeps around in by-streets, so as not to meet sympathizers in State Street."

After seeing Susie in a Christmas tableau he wrote, full of brotherly pride, that "Susie was really beautiful . . . everybody seemed to be looking at her, for I heard 'Susie Shaw' whispered all around me, and a shower of s's and sh's in the distance."

The winter was pleasant for Shaw. He took Susie for sleigh rides, skated often on the firelit ice of Fresh Pond. He was elected to the Hasty Pudding Club, went to concerts with Susie and his Forbes and Sturgis cousins and, once in a while, to the theater with a Boston girl. Slavery seemed far from his thoughts. There was no question in his mind that it was unjust, but his liberalism was, as yet, not fired in the heat of passion. Sometimes he went so far as to show irritation at the burgeoning zeal of antislavery leaders, his parents included. He felt he couldn't "talk and think of slavery all the time, and . . . I get tired (which I can't help) of hearing nothing else. . . ."

During his second year at Harvard, Shaw kept up a correspondence with his friends of Hanover days but expressed no longing to go back. Growing tired of Cambridge, he was fascinated by stories of men like John Charles Frémont and their fabled guides. He dreamed of settling in the West. A Hanover friend, a Philadelphian named Vezin, was a student of the latest agricultural methods. Shaw wrote Vezin suggesting that they form a partnership to buy ranch land out West. Shaw was drawn strongly to a life in the open.

Shaw's father, an amateur botanist, suggested that his son take a course in the subject. Shaw took his father's advice and found that he had an unexpected aptitude for this science. "It was rather singular that you should have recommended me to study that particularly, for we began it this term, and I take more interest in it than I ever did in any other study."

In September of 1858, after vacationing on Staten Island, with a hamper of apples, sandwiches and wine, Shaw boarded the "Empire State" with some of his classmates and traveled to Boston for his third and final year at Harvard. Plans for the ranching venture didn't work out. Shaw had had several chances to go into business, but of business life he had written from Europe, "I had rather be a chimney sweep. . . ." Now his feeling against a career in the world of commerce was less strong but his dreams were still the dreams of youth. He resisted letting go of them. But Shaw recognized that scholarship was not for him and, after Christmas, he began to give way in the face of pressure to go into the New York office of the mercantile firm of his uncle Henry P. Sturgis. "Uncle George advised me strongly to leave college and not let this opportunity go. . . . I am going to write Father about leaving college. . . ."

Shaw did leave Harvard before the end of his junior year, but he wrote a strong finish to his sojourn there. "I have been studying harder lately, because we are reviewing and have a good deal to do." Then, reluctantly admitting a reward of scholarship, perhaps thinking too of the sober days ahead, he continued, "I find I like Cambridge a great deal better. . . . I'm sure I don't know why—perhaps it is because I have been studying more . . . my marks last month were a good deal better than they had been before, and I think I shall improve on them this month. I shan't stand very high though at the end of the term."

5.

Shaw liked New York, a world of closely packed five-story red brick buildings, dwarfed by slim church steeples topped by gilded weathercocks. His were the days when dogs ran free in the streets, when the tip of the island was ringed by a crescent-shaped forest of masts and spars, the bowsprits of the steam frigates and sailing ships blackening the sky above West and South Streets.

But the routine of business life soon became tiresome. Shaw plodded away, in an unfamiliar style of life. He found little promise in his endeavors, lacked confidence in his ability to advance, yet found contentment too weak a brew for a man of his age. His charm, a shining asset in his travels in Europe and his days at Harvard, seemed to profit him little in a counting house. He lived sometimes in town, sometimes with his family on the green, low-lying island just across the bay. He savored the freedom of his Sundays and his after hours, but he was no better fitted for the world of business than for a life of scholarship.

In spring he was invited to spend a weekend with the Forbes family on Naushon Island. The rail terminal nearest Naushon was at New Bedford, Massachusetts, whose wharves on the west side of the harbor were hosts to the great whaling ships. Shaw was probably met at this busy port and sailed past the rocky points, bright dunes and sea grasses of Cape Cod into Hadley's Harbor to climb the hill and sign the guest book at the house where John Murray Forbes had taken up summer residence. Here Forbes entertained a constant stream of visitors. In a few short years he was to lend a hand in the recruiting of Negroes for Shaw's Fifty-Fourth Massachusetts Regiment.

Wilting in his New York office, Shaw took comfort in the hope that business might give him a chance to travel. In July he wrote in German to his friend Heinrich, then on an expedition to Central America, "I am in the East India business, as perhaps you have heard, and I may go to China some time within two or three years in which case I want first to go to England, Germany, or Norway in summer, and from there through Siberia, in winter to China."

Shaw suggested that by then Heinrich might be home in Germany, that it might be pleasant for them to visit their old haunts together and perhaps travel through Siberia; "That road is traveled a good deal now, I believe, by Russian merchants. . . .

"I wish I were with you, as you say, in Central America: but I shall never travel again unless on some sort of business or other. . . ."

Shaw crossed the bay often to be with his family, and sometimes he stayed on Staten Island. The trip from Battery Park, where New Yorkers took the salt air on clear days, was pleasant indeed. The ferry terminal was like a white-painted doll's house; there was a cupola in the center of its roof, flanked by flags, and over the entry, a portico. The ferry itself was a small side-wheeler with ample deck space, providing the passengers with a fine view of the bustling harbor, which swarmed with sailing ships and steamers plying their coastwise trade or sailing to and from distant ports. Sometimes Shaw was met at Thompkinsville Landing, sometimes traveled the dusty shore road in a rattling horsecar with a tentlike roof to Davis Avenue, where the Shaws had bought a piece of land and built a house. Their plot in West New Brighton was in Dr. Elliott's tailor-made village, Elliottville. Elliott's own mansion dominated the village, and in front of his house was a large formal garden laced over with pleasant paths.

Again Shaw wrote Heinrich, who had decided to stop off in the United States on his way back to Europe. Heinrich planned to join a deer hunt during his visit and wanted to wangle Shaw an invitation. Shaw wrote mournfully, "How I would like to go on that deer-hunt. But I am a slave now and, even if I were invited, I could not go."

Heinrich's mother and sister had been lost in the burning of the *Austria*, and Shaw wrote words of comfort and advice. "It is rather absurd of me, who have never experienced any real misfortune, to speak to you about it (your grief) or to give you any advice; but it seems to me that you ought to think as much as possible of the future, and seek diversion as much as possible. I should try to think as little of it as possible until you are able to do so with a peaceful mind."

Shaw's interest in politics quickened in the summer of 1860, as the Presidential campaign gathered force. Shaw, as was natural, gave his support to Abraham Lincoln. In New York it was a time for bright banners and marching bands, for floats and fireworks. Though Lincoln, in his travels, made short, almost reluctant speeches, the voices of his champions rent the air. William Henry Seward, who had been defeated by Lincoln for the nomination, was by far the most active Republican campaigner. He traveled tirelessly and delivered brilliant speeches.

Shaw, the young man in the street, his straw hat worn at a slight angle, a thin cigar in his teeth, listened to the speeches and in the evenings, with his friends, watched torchlight parades.

A man who had no particular love for Douglas came to New York to press for the defeat of Lincoln. William Lowndes Yancy, the deceptively mild-mannered secessionist leader, added sparks to the raging campaign on October 10 when he made a long speech often interrupted by applause and laughter. Yancy protested his belief in the Constitution, he excoriated "Black Republicans" and Abolitionists. Referring to slavery, his language was particularly pungent. "So then, gentlemen, this institution is necessary to your prosperity as well as to ours. It is an institution, too, that doesn't harm you, for we don't let our niggers run about to injure anybody (laughter); we keep them; they never steal from you; they don't trouble you even with that peculiar stench, which is very good in the nose of the Southern man, but intolerable in the nose of a Northerner."

In November, the twenty-three-year old Shaw cast his first and only Presidential vote, and his spirits jumped mast-high when Lincoln won. He knew, as everyone seemed to know, that trouble lay ahead, but soon after the election he took a holiday from work . . . forgot about his discontent and his country's troubles. He went to Boston and then to Niagara and Toronto. Traveling alone from Boston to Albany, Shaw met a little Scotsman who was going shooting on the prairies. "He had a very broad brogue, and the most good-natured, jolly face in the world. At Albany we walked about the city arm-in-arm as if we had been old friends. He has a travelling name—Jackson; but his real name is McLean. A novel idea isn't it? He says it's common in England. He is a very intelligent and very funny little man, and only laughs at the peculiarities of our countrymen. In the Delevan House at Albany, a gentleman near us emitted a very loud and unequivocal belch. . . . Mr. J. laughed a great deal and said: 'Let your manners be simple and 'asy.' He says, though, that he has seen pretty bad manners among Englishmen—for instance, a sea captain whom he sailed with used always to wipe his fork on his hair before asking his passengers if he could help them to a little more pork. . . ."

Shaw's brother-in-law, George Curtis,[1] who was on a lecture tour of the Northeast and Canada, joined Shaw and traveled with him for a while. Curtis was a distinguished scholar and popular speaker. He had a long, pleasant face decorated by copious sideburns. Curtis and Shaw were fast friends.

The Scot went with them part way to Toronto—bidding good-by to them at a point where they changed cars. "We were sorry to lose his company; he was so full of Scottish legends and poetry, and told so many pleasant anecdotes of his travels."

At Toronto, Curtis delivered a lecture on the work of Dickens. "After the lecture they gave us a little entertainment consisting of beer and oysters, which we enjoyed very much."

In March, as the bubble of peace was about to burst, Shaw's father and mother sailed south in rough seas on the small steamer *Karnak* to vacation in Nassau and Havana. While his family were gone, Shaw spent most of his weekends and some of his evenings on Staten Island. One of his uncles had given him the responsibility of renting his house to a suitable tenant. Shaw refused one prospect because he had a brother-in-law from New Orleans who would be in residence part of the time. "We don't want any secessionists about. . . ." Shaw spent pleasant evenings with friends and relations. One evening, with an unnamed escort, he went to the dazzling Winter Garden, with its curving balcony and sparkling chandeliers, to see Edwin Booth and Charlotte Cushman perform in Macbeth. "It was really splendid. The house was jammed from top to bottom."

---

[1] George W. Curtis, married to Shaw's sister Anna, was an author and lecturer of winning style. He was an intimate of James Russell Lowell. In his younger days he had spent two years at Brook Farm. He was a deeply idealistic man who had developed a hatred of slavery. In 1863, he would become the editor of *Harper's Weekly*.

Writing to his father, Shaw said, "You will see from the papers conflicting rumors we have had about the evacuation of Fort Sumter. Nobody knows as yet what is going to be done. They say that Fort Pickens is to be re-enforced by 400 men. I hope it is true. If they do that and evacuate Sumter, it will be just what you wanted."

The elder Shaw favored the evacuation of Sumter and the holding of Pickens (at the entrance to Pensacola Harbor) because Pickens was easily reinforceable from the sea whereas Sumter, set in the entrance to the strongly fortified port of Charleston, was in a very different position. Lincoln was reluctant to blast his way into Charleston, since seven of the eight slave states remaining in the Union would forthwith be blasted into the Confederacy. Of the remaining slave states, only Delaware was considered safe.

In March of that year, heavy snows fell on Manhattan. The snowstorms were followed by leaden skies and torrents of rain. The streets were slushy, and Shaw, unable to enjoy his customary walks, missing his family and bored by his labors in his uncle's firm, suffered acutely from low spirits. When the load of depression was somewhat lightened, he wrote his parents. "I didn't say anything to Mr. Robbins about my affairs until last week, and then he asked me to go to his house some evening and have a talk with him. So on Saturday I went. We had a very nice talk; and he said he thought I was mistaken in thinking I wasn't fitted for business . . . that if I had more confidence in myself I should get along a good deal better. He says when he went to India, and first received orders to load a ship, he felt like jumping into the sea, and expected to be called home as soon as they found out what he had bought."

In the same letter, evincing a lively interest in the coming storm and in the personality of the newly elected President, Shaw wrote, "We have been in a great state of excitement about Fort Sumter. First it was to be evacuated, then re-enforced. The other day, a messenger had been sent from Lincoln to Major Anderson,[2] and the next day he had not. From the many conflicting reports, I infer that Mr. Lincoln is sharp enough to keep his plans to himself, and leave the papers to guess what is going on."

In fact, though he felt that force must eventually be used, Lin-

---

[2] Major Robert Anderson, born in Kentucky and with roots in Virginia, was proslavery in sentiment and believed secession inevitable though he hoped that the seceding states could be brought back into the Union at a

coln was not at all certain about what course to take. Shaw commented on Seward's view of Lincoln. "I heard from Mr. Schuyler last night that Mr. Seward had said to some of their family last week that Mr. Lincoln was a pure, honest-minded, patriotic man, and that whatever he did would be for the good of the country. And this gentleman says it is remarkable to see what an impression Mr. Lincoln has made upon Mr. Seward. They say that the office-seekers, and people who are slightly acquainted with him, think he is nothing but a joker and after-dinner story teller, because they can't get him to say anything on important subjects. . . ."

Shaw had some harsh words for the British. "The London *Times*, which at first went for the North, has turned round since the passage of the Tarriff Bill, and says we shall sink into nothing, and the South grow great and prosperous in proportion. If the *Times* is the exponent of the popular voice, as it pretends to be, it shows that the English people go for the right as long as it doesn't interfere with their pockets. . . ."

On April 5, just one week before Fort Sumter was fired on, Shaw, seeming to sense that events transpiring would give his life direction and meaning, wrote with quickening pulse to his beloved Susie who was still in Cambridge, "We have exciting news today from the South. It is now almost certain that Mr. Lincoln is going to re-enforce the United States forts, and in that case the Southerners will almost surely resist. All the vessels of the Navy are being got ready for sea, and several sail from here to-day. Lincoln kept his own counsel so well hitherto that the newspapers have not been able to get at anything, and have consequently been filled with the most extraordinary rumors. But, now that almost all the important appointments have been made, and the State elections, &c. are over, it is the universal belief that *something* decisive is to be done. . . .

"For my part I want to see the Southern States either brought back by force, or else recognized as independent. . . ."

Quite naturally taking Lincoln's side in his interpretation of the Constitution and convinced, as Lincoln was convinced, that abandonment of the Union was an anarchistic act, but apparently un-

---

later date. He was loyal to the Federal government. He was occupying Sumter when it was fired on at the start of the war. He defended Sumter for thirty-four hours until forced to capitulate. After Anderson's evacuation of Sumter, his health began to decline. After a short stint of command in Kentucky, where he helped save that state for the Union, he was relieved. He retired before the end of the war.

aware of Lincoln's reluctance to be cast in the role of aggressor, Shaw wrote, "as Lincoln cannot do what he likes, but must abide by the Constitution, I don't see what he can do but collect revenue and re-take, by force of arms, the United States property which they have stolen. As for making concessions, it is only patching the affair up for a year or two, when it would break out worse than ever. At any rate we should have the same row over again at every Presidential election; and if we give them an inch they would be sure to want thousands of ells, as is proven by their history and ours for the last 50 years. Indeed, they would not be content with anything less than a total change of public opinion throughout the North on the subject of slavery, and that of course they cannot have. . . . I have been a Disunionist for two years;[3] but, as there seems to be no way of making a peaceable separation without giving up everything, I am glad for the credit of the country that they will probably act with some firmness. A great many people say they are ashamed of their country but I feel proud that we have at last taken such a long step forward as to turn out the pro-slavery government which has been disgracing us for so long. . . ."

In the same letter, Shaw sympathized with Lincoln and his cabinet, noting that, in a government cumbersome even then, everything couldn't be done at once "even if they had machines to make Ambassadors, Postmasters, Collectors of ports . . . besides besieging forts, building ships, recruiting the army, and picking out officers that won't turn traitor as many have done."

So that he wouldn't be left behind if war did start, Shaw had joined the Seventh Regiment of the New York State Militia and had drilled in the evenings at the Seventh's armory, then above Tompkins Market in Lafayette Place.

At 4:30 on the morning of April 12, a mortar was fired from Fort Johnson, its shell arching through the night, exploding directly above the fort and signaling the start of the war. In the following days, the buildings of New York echoed the newsboys' frantic cries.

On April 15, Lincoln called for 75,000 men to rush to the defense of Washington. New York's Seventh was one of the first to respond.

---

[3] Shaw seems to have been a Disunionist for more than two years. In the fall of 1858, he had written from Cambridge, "I can't help hoping there will be disunion at some time. . . ." (See p. 17 *supra*.)

6.

The Seventh boasted an illustrious membership, many of them men of wealth and social position. The regiment, formed at a meeting on an August evening in 1824 at the old Shakespeare Tavern at Fulton and Nassau Streets, was the pride of the city. "The National Guards," as it had originally been called, had been used to putting down such civil disturbances as the Astor Place riots, surprisingly started in May of 1859 as a demonstration against the British rival of an American actor.

On the eighteenth, Shaw sat down at a desk in the family home on Staten Island and penned three letters. To his father he wrote:

> My dear Father,
>   When you get home you will hear why I am here to receive you. Badly as I feel at going before you come, it seems the only way, unless I give it up altogether, which you could not wish, any more than I. You shall hear from me as often as I possibly can write, if only a few words at a time. We go off tomorrow afternoon, and hope to be in Washington the following day. I want very much to go, and with me, as with most others, the only hard part is leaving our friends.
>   God bless you all, dear Father! Excuse the shortness of this farewell note, as I am busy getting things ready. I shall write Susie to-day. Give my love to dear Effie and Nellie. I would write them if I had time.
>
> Your ever loving son,
ROBERT G. SHAW.

To his mother Shaw wrote in part, "We all feel that, if we can get to Washington before Virginia begins to make trouble, we shall not have much fighting. . . . The Massachusetts men passed through New York this morning. . . . Won't it be grand to meet the men from all the States, East and West, down there ready to fight for the country, as the old fellows did in the Revolution?

"I came down this morning to see Anna before I go. She and the new baby look finely. . . ." Shaw's Colonel was Marshall Lefferts. "Our colonel tells us we are only going to Washington for the present, and shall be sent back to New York as soon as troops from the more distant states can arrive."

Shaw wrote to his sister, "You mustn't think, dear Sue, that any of us are going to be killed; for they are collecting such a force there that an attack would be insane,—that is, unless the Southerners can get their army up in an impossibly short space of time."

The weather was fine the following day. The counting rooms and workshops were deserted. Men stood in the streets in knots, talking of days that lay ahead. Other soldiers had passed through the streets of the city, but this was the day when, for New York, the war would begin in earnest. The stars and stripes flew from poles on the houses and churches, over store windows holding fresh frocks in the style of the day and snapped in the breeze on factories and ships at their piers or riding at anchor in the great harbor.

The time of the Seventh's departure had been noised abroad and by noon a million people thronged the line of march. There were children wearing tricolored streamers, stevedores and barmaids, printers in their paper hats, ladies with silk shawls and lace at their throats and gentlemen come to shout their praise of the city's proudest regiment.

At Tompkins Market, carriages pressed through the throng bringing members of the regiment and their families to the bulging armory. Publication of the orders to march had brought a flood of recruits, but by now the regiment was nearly 1,000 strong and the tardy patriots were turned away in droves. In a sentimental age, sentiment flourished like ragweed in July. Wives and sweethearts came with hampers of sandwiches, cordials and comforts for the march. Women thrust into the hands of their dear ones little bouquets labeled in gold, "May peace bring you back to me." Fathers proudly presented their sons with dirks and pistols to protect them on their march through seething Baltimore. Mr. Robbins gave Shaw a fine revolver. Marvelously Victorian phrases were heard above the din, "I'll come back promoted, Father, or I won't come at all" and "Mother gave me this little flag, God bless her. I'll never disgrace it."

Shaw wore his stiffly new private's uniform—blue overcoat and gray, black-trimmed suit and cap. And with his knapsack full of gifts from Mr. Robbins, friends and relatives, he joined his company, listened to some parting speeches and took his rifle off the rack.

Just before the start of the march, news was received of the attack, that morning, on the Sixth Massachusetts in Baltimore. Blood had been shed.[1] The news brought firm resolve on the part of the soldiers of the Seventh to march through Baltimore at all costs.

At three o'clock came the roll of the drums and a mammoth van, gaily decked with flags and carrying baggage, emerged from the armory. There were thunderous cheers as the regiment moved into Lafayette Place, led by the brightly clad Zouaves in their flaming red shirts and billowing trousers, closely followed by two brass twelve-pounders, polished to a fare-thee-well, kicking the sunlight into watching eyes.

A week later Shaw would write to Sue, "Our march down Broadway was a thing I shall never forget. . . . The people would hardly let us pass. . . ." Shaw was the flank man of his platoon. The people caught hold of his hand, slapped him on the back, "yelling and screaming like wild men."

Overhead was a canopy of flags and streamers. Throngs overrunning the sidewalks, bulging through police lines and surging into the street were driven back at the point of the bayonet. Windows were choked with madly cheering men and women, children perched on bunting-covered lamp posts and rooftops, and all along the line of march there were thunderous cheers, picked up ahead and dying slowly as the regiment passed. Handkerchiefs fluttered down like flights of butterflies, and "pretty little gloves pelted us with love taps."

Major Anderson, late of Sumter, appeared on the balcony of Ball, Black & Co., and was cheered roundly by Shaw and his regimental fellows. A man who marched with Shaw wrote, "It was worth a life, that march. Only one who passed, as we did, through that tempest of cheers, two miles long, can know the terrible enthusiasm of the occasion. I could hardly hear the rattle of

---

[1] The march of the Sixth Massachusetts through Baltimore occasioned a full-scale riot in which four soldiers were killed and thirty-six wounded. Twelve civilians were killed and countless civilians wounded. Some of the latter were rioters, some were innocent bystanders. This was the first bloodshed of the war.

our own gun carriages, and only twice the music of our band came to me, muffled and quelled by the uproar."

About 5:30, swinging at last away from Broadway into lavishly garlanded Cortlandt Street, the men of the regiment pressed through the tightly packed crowds to board the ferry which moved away from Dock Eighteen to the ear-splitting shrill of hundreds of whistles and the clanging of the bells of tugs, steamers and sailing ships that swarmed across the broad, flat surface of the Hudson River.

Bonfires blazed along the railroad track that night as the rocking cars of the New Jersey Railroad took the men of the Seventh south. Dispatches were sent back to New York by telegraph, announcing the passage of the regiment through the cities and farming villages, where people kept a vigil in the night. Women came to city stations and whistle stops laden with boxes of sandwiches, cookies and pots of hot coffee, men pressed pints of whiskey and cedar boxes of cigars into the hands of the soldier boys. As the bottles were emptied, songs were begun. The regiment was met in the cities by resounding cheers and flaming torches. The ladies of Burlington came with pails of iced water and tin cups and, in the wee small hours, the train rolled across the Delaware and into Broad Street Depot in the city of Philadelphia.

As soon as the city began to stir, its people did the soldiers proud. One man remembered that when they arrived, "a mountain of bread was already piled up in the station. I stuck my bayonet through a stout loaf, and, with a dozen comrades armed in the same way, went about foraging for other vivres. It is a poor part of Philadelphia; but whatever they had in the shops or the houses seemed to be at our disposition."

Colonel Lefferts, after some deliberation, decided that, since the primary objective was to speed his men to Washington, he should bypass the city of Baltimore. Not only had there been riots and bloodshed in Baltimore, but railroad bridges between Havre de Grace and Baltimore had been put to the torch and sections of track had been torn up. Artillery and barricades had been set up by Secessionists at strategic points in the strife-torn city. There was a ferry at Havre de Grace but Lefferts, disagreeing with Brigadier General Ben Butler, whom Shaw described as "an energetic, cursing and swearing old fellow," felt that dependence on such a mode of transportation would be unwise. Lefferts felt, quite rightly, that the ferry could easily be sabotaged. Butler had tried to pull rank and take the Seventh under his wing but Lefferts would have none of him, arguing that neither regiment was, as yet, in the service of the Federal government. Lefferts decided that the best route would be through Annapolis, so he chartered the freighter *Boston* which, after five hours' work by Philadelphia stevedores, was delivered of her cargo. Butler, meanwhile, had decided to follow Lefferts's example and take his regiment by sea.

Lefferts's men were packed like sardines in a can, but the weather was clear and it was warm for April. Shaw huddled with the men of his company on one of the wooden upper decks as day gave way to a soft, starry night. The talk, of course, was all of war and there were wild rumors of sweeping Southern victories and the scuttling of the entire Federal navy. Poetry burned in the breast of many a soldier and natural laws were suspended that night. "The moon rose with matchless beauty to complete the scene; and the rugged mate of the steamer, glancing toward it, saw three distinct and beautiful circles surrounding it,—red, white and blue! 'There,' he cried, 'is our flag in the sky! God will never let it be struck down under foot!'"

Life was not much aboard the *Boston*. According to Shaw the meat was "horsey," water was scarce and sleeping difficult. "When we wanted to make a turn we would all have to wake up and turn together." Some men didn't sleep at all and there was soft singing through the night.

The *Boston* made her way down the Delaware into the Atlantic. Chesapeake Bay was entered, and the lifting of the morning mists revealed the roofs and spires of Annapolis, rising above the farms and plantations of the Maryland countryside. The frigate *Constitution*, then used as a training ship for middies, was anchored off shore and the *Maryland*, carrying Butler's regiment, was hard aground. Shaw wrote that the grounding was intentional, that the pilot, "whom they immediately put in irons and wanted to kill" was a Secessionist.

The Massachusetts men had jettisoned baggage trucks and crates and some of their luggage and had rushed in unison from side to side to dislodge their prison, but all to no avail. At high tide, the *Boston* tried to tow the *Maryland* free, but finally, after unloading her cargo of troops, she stood close to the *Maryland* and took the men off.

Shaw had something of a holiday at Annapolis. The midshipmen, in their natty blues, treated the soldiers well. Shaw had a bath and, in the evening, lay on the grass with the men of his company and listened to the music of the regimental band. In a postscript to a letter home, Shaw said, "Hope to see Old Abe soon."

Before dawn on Wednesday morning, April 24, the Seventh marched for Annapolis Junction some thirty miles west on the main line from Baltimore to Washington. In a flat, wooded section a raiding party scattered at the approach of the Seventh, but though the regiment fully expected to be assaulted or at least harassed and though Shaw observed, "we went into a good many defiles where the Marylanders might have pounced upon us with great advantage," there was, in fact, no attack on the column. But the sun as it blazed in a citron sky, and the gorges whose walls would admit no breezes, proved formidable enemies in themselves.

The night brought sudden cold and a moon that glinted on burnished bayonets. At last, after pressing forward with very little rest, the regiment reached the junction. A great bonfire was built of fence rails and the men foraged for food at surrounding farms. Shaw wrote that he breakfasted at a nearby farm. "The lady of the house was a real pretty, nice woman, and, though she seemed frightened at first, was soon reassured, and furnished us hoe-cake, pork, bread and butter, potatoes, coffee, tea and milk in abundance. This worked a wonderful change in us. . . ."

The regiment boarded a train in the charge of the "National Rifles" under Captain Smead and departed at ten, reaching Washington at noon. "Then we were turned out for a parade just as we were, covered with dust, and with our blankets slung over our shoulders. . . ." Shaw continued his report of the march, "straight up to the White House and through the grounds, where 'Old Abe' and family stood at the doors and saw us go by."

A dispatch, filed by a *Tribune* reporter on the day of arrival of the Seventh, said of the regiment's march down Pennsylvania Avenue, "When in place of the drums and fifes, the full band struck up, the whole city danced with delight." Of the President the reporter wrote, "Mr. Lincoln was the happiest-looking man in town as the regiment was marching by him. As an Illinois man remarked, 'He smiled all over. . . .' "

Some of the Seventh's companies were quartered at Willard's, Brown's and the National Hotel. But Shaw's company, with a few others, was quartered in the House of Representatives, where Shaw appropriated one of the desks and slept on the floor. He wrote, "I have no doubt that we are the best-behaved Congress that has been in session for a good while. . . ."[2]

The following day, under a cloudless sky, there was a ceremony swearing the men of regiment into the service of the Federal government for thirty days. Shaw wrote, "Old Abe stood out in front of us, looking as pleasant and kind as possible, and, when we presented arms, took off his hat in the most awkward way, putting it on again with his hand on the back of the rim, country fashion. A boy came up with a pail of water for us, and the President took a great swig from it as it passed. I couldn't help thinking of the immense responsibility he has on his shoulders, as he stood there laughing and talking." In another account of the same ceremony Shaw wrote that Lincoln's two boys were there, that he was holding them by the hand and, "when he laughs he doubles himself up. . . ."

Shaw took his meals with members of his company at various hotels, but after the swearing-in ceremony, he and his fellow inhabitants of the Capitol building found that in the rotunda a great mass of provender was being distributed by a squad of men. A reporter enumerated: "15 kegs of lager beer, 2000 boiled eggs, piles of cheese, boxes of lemons and oranges, smoked beef, pipes and tobacco, etc." It was clear that the people of Washington meant to take care of their soldier boys.

Shaw had leave one afternoon to wander about the city's rutted streets. All the bridges were heavily guarded and precautions had been taken to guard against landings by boat or raft or the upper and lower banks of the Potomac River. Earthworks had been thrown up around the city, the public buildings were barricaded and howitzers mounted on either side of the rear entrance of the Capitol

[2] Shaw was probably thinking of the caning of Charles Sumner by Preston Brooks on the floor of the Senate.

building, the front entrance being closed. Shaw found that the city, "with the exception of the White House grounds, and some other public buildings, is a pretty poor place."

All things considered, Shaw's duty was pleasant enough. He stood guard, did his share of a private's menial chores. The grounds of the Capitol were pleasant and trees were in bloom about the city, giving off a delicious fragrance.

On April 30, Shaw paid a call on Abraham Lincoln. He wrote, "On Tuesday, King[3] asked me to go with him to see Mr. Seward; so we got leave to go out for the afternoon, and walked up to the War Department. King knew him very well, and we had a little talk with him. He gave me the impression of being a pretty sly old fellow, and really didn't look as if he could have written those great speeches. We told him we should like very much to see the President; so he gave us a note to him, and off we trotted to make a call. After waiting a few minutes in an antechamber, we were shown into a room where Mr. Lincoln was sitting at a desk perfectly covered with papers of every description. He got up and shook hands with us both, in the most cordial way, asked us to be seated, and seemed quite glad to have us come. It is really too bad to call him one of the ugliest men in the country, for I have seldom seen a pleasanter or more kind-hearted looking one, and he has certainly a very striking face. It is easy to see why he is so popular with all who come into contact with him. His voice is very pleasant; and, though to be sure we were only there a few minutes, I didn't hear anything like a Western slang or twang in him. He gives you the impression, too, of being a gentleman. I told him I had heard of his son at Cambridge; and we talked a little about our regiment. . . ." Shaw continued, "Though you can't judge of a man in a five minutes' conversation, we were very much pleased with what we saw of him. We got rather ahead of the rest of the regiment, as none of the others have seen him, and thought we did a pretty good afternoon's work in calling on the President and Secretary of State."

While he was in Washington, Shaw decided to stay in the army at least until it was clear what course the war would take. Feeling that there was no shortage of enlisted men, that he was qualified to be an officer, he applied for a commission in a Massachusetts

[3] Rufus King, son of Charles King, president of Columbia College, was a private in Shaw's company (Sixth Company under Captain Nevers).

regiment. He wrote his mother, "I don't want to go without a commission though I would do so without any hesitation if there were a lack of men."

On the afternoon of May 2, the Seventh went into camp on Meridian Hill, two miles east of the White House on the road to Harper's Ferry. Shaw stayed behind in the House of Representatives with a detail of about twenty-five men, to sweep up the place. He wrote of the work that "such a dust as we raised you never saw. There was an astonishing amount of dirt there, and it took as much as two hours to scatter it about, so that it seemed to me to look much worse than it had before."

The first day in camp was marked by torrential rains and the men slept in wet blankets in their floorless tents. But when the weather cleared, most of them were happy to be living in the open. When the expected attack on Washington failed to materialize, the troops became restive and Shaw wrote, "we have lost sight of what we came for and seem to be on a grand picnic."

Major Anderson, who, in spite of his lionization by the citizens of New York, was rather a tragic figure, came to the camp on Meridian Hill. Shaw saw him walking about the camp. "He seemed unwell and looked quite said."

On May 11 Shaw received the news that he had been commissioned a second lieutenant in the Second Massachusetts. He left his regiment and traveled north.

7.

Shaw arrived at Camp Andrew in West Roxbury on May 18, having been commissioned on the tenth, while still in camp on Meridian Hill. The Massachusetts Second, one of the early regiments enlisting its men for three years or the duration of the war, was forming and training on the site where Brook Farm had stood and Shaw felt very much at home there. The camp consisted of a great pattern of tents on the side of a grass-covered hill. Headquarters had been established in a nearby farmhouse. Second growth flourished close to the encampment and, on lower ground, there were patches of woodland. The Second was the first and last regiment to camp on the site, and the ground was untrampled and clean. Shaw's company pitched their tents where the Pilgrim House had stood. Every day Shaw saw something that reminded him of the "Community days." He wrote, "The road through the woods is just as it used to be, and I found some quartz in the same place we used to get it, fourteen years ago, to strike sparks from."

Shaw's senior officers were Colonel George H. Gordon and Lieutenant Colonel George L. Andrews, both graduates of the United States Military Academy at West Point. Gordon was a handsome man with a prominent nose and deep-set eyes. He prided himself on his youthful appearance. He was a strict disciplinarian though he had in his nature a poetic strain. Andrews, who had been graduated from West Point in '51, five years later than Gordon, was balding, looked older and lacked Gordon's dash. Gordon brooked no nonsense. One of his captains, seen raising a fraternal cup with an enlisted man, was reprimanded and asked to leave the regiment. Knowing Gordon's expectations, Shaw must have had some uncomfortable moments learning to handle the raw recruits, many of whom were brought in "more or less drunk."

Shaw's cousin and childhood friend, Harry Russell, was one of the officers of the new regiment, and Shaw met three others at camp who would be special friends. Of these, Henry Higginson and

Greely Curtis, whom Shaw later described as the boldest man he knew, would leave the Second, but Charles F. Morse would be an almost constant companion of Shaw until Shaw left to command the Fifty-Fourth.

June was warm and pleasant. Shaw drilled with his company, studied military science, did his share of paper work, found time to visit friends and relatives in Boston and attend Class Day at Harvard.

Spring passed in a kaleidoscopic round of daily duties and preparations for farewell parades. "We appeared yesterday in our United States felt hats and cut a very funny figure."

Shaw rode out with Greely Curtis and the quartermaster to practice forming a wagon train. "The whole of West Roxbury turned out as we rattled through; and Greely and I galloped in front, feeling as if we were leading a brigade. We left the train, after a while, and turned up the lane where Aunt Follen used to live and cut across to our old house. The trees have grown very large and it is really a beautiful place now."

In anticipation of his passage through New York, Shaw wrote to his mother to reserve rooms at the Fifth Avenue Hotel so that his family could be in the city the day the regiment arrived. On the eighth of July, the regiment went to Boston and paraded through the streets before entraining for Groton, Connecticut where they boarded a steamer for a moonlit ride to New York. Shaw visited his family as planned, and there was an unexpected bit of excitement for him when the side-wheeler bearing the regiment crossed the upper bay in the late afternoon and pointed toward Kill Van Kull. Shaw's parents and sisters had wasted no time in taking the ferry for Staten Island. The troopship passed close to the ferry as it crossed the bay and Shaw stood on the paddle box and waved to his family— his father in sober black, his mother and sisters in their summer finery of delicate pink and white and powder blue as they waved their handkerchiefs in the breeze. Boarding the train at Elizabeth Port, Shaw slept through the night on a pile of straw in a baggage car. The cars jogged and rattled through flat New Jersey farms and into central Pennsylvania, passing blazing iron furnaces of the Lehigh Valley just at dawn, making for Harrisburg as the sun beat down on the deep wheat fields of the Cumberland Valley. At Harrisburg, the cars rolled over the Susquehanna and on southwest along the curving valley into Hagerstown, Maryland. Shaw stood guard through the night on the station platform until the regiment formed and marched to the banks of the Potomac at Williamsport. The fording of the river was picturesque: the men and white-topped baggage trains, the glistening waters, the sounds of the regimental band and the shouted commands.

At Martinburg, Virginia, the regiment reported to the headquarters of General Robert Patterson. Three days after the arrival of the regiment at Martinburg, Patterson moved out toward Confederate General Joseph E. Johnston who was in camp at Bunker Hill in the Shenandoah Valley. Colonel Gordon wrote a thumping description of the breaking of camp, ending with an account of civilized behavior that would not outlast the beginning of the war. "While the tents were being packed, while wagons filled the parade ground and luggage encumbered the earth; while there was motion everywhere, as far as the eye could see,—galloping horses bearing orderlies with dispatches, artillery rumbling, and long lines of infantry moving out to the inspiring militia-muster melody of jingling kettledrums, screeching fifes, and roaring bass,—a sharp-featured and sombre person, dressed in the prevailing butternut-colored homespun of Virginia, shying up toward the Colonel of the Second Massachusetts Regiment, demanded a settlement: first for the fence rails we had burned; second for the grass we had trampled down; and third for an extra cost of ploughing in the coming spring, the soil had been trodden down so hard."

The Virginian was paid in gold and the regiment moved south toward Charlestown where, two years before, John Brown of Ossawatomie had been tried and hung. During the march, Shaw saw, for the first time, the grandeur of the Shenandoah Valley which had seemed like the promised land to the Scotch-Irish and German settlers who had come there from Pennsylvania in the 1730's. In summer the place was green, clear to the tops of the mountains. The fields and orchards that stretched away to the south would bear heavy harvests in the fall. In the coming year, Shaw would come to know the valley well.

Patterson, who was sixty-nine years old and a veteran of the War of 1812, had been told to keep General Johnston busy so that he couldn't join forces with General Beauregard at Manassas Junction where the first battle of Bull Run was soon to be written into history.

Patterson was expected to make warlike movements, but he was never told in so many words to engage the enemy. He had, in fact, been told not to take unnecessary risks. His advance guard fought a skirmish with J. E. B. Stuart's cavalry and Patterson moved south. As Johnston withdrew to join Beauregard, Patterson was left to decide whether to pursue his elusive enemy or withdraw. His force was weaker than it should have been and, all things considered, it is not surprising that he decided it would be folly to advance further.

The morning of the eighteenth, a few days before Bull Run, found the Massachusetts Second marching into Harper's Ferry, the regiment's commander having been ordered to occupy and "assume command of" the town. Patterson himself was close by with the rest of his force, far from the scene of the first big battle of the Civil War. Patterson's reputation would become one of the casualties of the confusion that reigned as the war began.

As the regiment marched into town it was greeted with cheers and garlands of flowers by the Unionist citizens. These were the first Federal soldiers to enter the town since the withdrawal, at the start of the war, of Lieutenant Roger Jones and his company of forty men.

Shaw found Harper's Ferry, at the confluence of the Potomac and Shenandoah Rivers, an enchanting place, made more so by the presence of the ghost of the great hero of the New England anti-slavery community. The rivers ran through deep gorges and the town had been built on the peninsula formed by the joining of the waters. A wide, covered railroad bridge had crossed the Potomac from the Maryland side, but the bridge had been burned by Jones and his men when they had fled the town three months before. The railroad tracks of the western line of the Baltimore and Ohio Railroad, now broken at the bridge, ran along the south shore of the Potomac until the river curved north a mile or so west of the town. Near the tip of the peninsula, by the railroad track, stood the engine house of the United States armory, within whose walls John Brown had made his last stand. The building's smokestack towered above the other structures along the river. The armory became the regimental guardhouse. Shaw described the place in a letter to his sister, Susie. "There are three or four loopholes which he made to fire through, and marks of musket balls on the walls inside. It seems the worst place he could have chosen to defend against an attack; for when the doors are shut, it is like a brick box, as all the windows are high up, and the loopholes are so small that they give no range at all to the men firing through them."

Beyond the islands that poked above the surface of the Potomac, the little schoolhouse, where Brown had hidden rifles sent him by Massachusetts donors, could be clearly seen beside the canal on the Maryland side.

In our time, John Brown is often dismissed as a murdering, maniacal devil who rose out of a sleepy Connecticut town and streaked across the nation's horizon like an evil bolt of summer lightning. Shaw, however, as well as elder members of the antislavery community and people on its fringes, saw him as a towering martyr. To the people who had devoted their lives to the destruction of the "peculiar institution," Brown was a great idealist who had lived by the sword because he believed that only by the sword could the black man be freed.

On Saturday evening, November 18, 1859, in Boston's Tremont Temple, as Brown had languished in Charlestown jail, a meeting had been held to enlist aid for Brown's family "in their poverty and distress." The meeting had been addressed by John A. Andrew, who had contributed time and money to Brown's defense. Wendell Phillips and Ralph Waldo Emerson had spoken. Their words that night had attested to their untarnished admiration for Brown. Andrew had said, "John Brown and his companions in the conflict at Harper's Ferry, those who fell and those who are to suffer upon the scaffold, are victims or martyrs to an idea. There is an irresistible conflict between freedom and slavery, as old and as immortal as the irresistible conflict between right and wrong. They are martyrs of that conflict."

Emerson had asserted, "Indeed, it is the *reductio ad absurdum* of slavery, when the Governor of Virginia is forced to hang a man whom he declares to be a man of the most integrity, truthfulness and courage he has ever met. Is that the kind of man the gallows is built for? It were bold to affirm that there is within that broad Commonwealth, at this moment, another citizen as worthy to live, and as deserving of all public and private honor, as this poor prisoner."

Wendell Phillips had mounted the podium amid tumultuous

cheers and had given a speech in which he praised Brown's character. He presented Brown as a family man, never intemperate or
profane. He praised his work. "Could we ask a better symbol for
history?" Phillips suggested that a message be sent to Brown from
his supporters in Boston. "We lay your wife and children in the
very corner of our hearts. . . ." He predicted, "The whole world will
yet ring with the heroism of his attempt. He has opened a light
upon the Bastille of America." Quoting Brown, Phillips's voice rang
out, "We have given the sword to the white man; the time has come
to give it to the black!"

After the disaster at Bull Run, General McClellan was called to
Washington from western Virginia and asked by Lincoln to bring
some order into the chaos that reigned around Washington. George
Brinton McClellan was only thirty-five and he had served his country well both before the war and in its early stages. He had been
a brilliant student at West Point, had been decorated for bravery
in the Mexican War, had been an official observer at Sevastopol in
the Crimean War and had taken a turn as president of the Eastern
Division of the Ohio and Mississippi Railroad. As commander of
the Department of the Ohio at the start of the war he had secured
control of western Virginia for the Federal government. McClellan's
performance had won him the respect of the Lincoln Administration
and the adulation of the soldiers in his command. He arrived in
Washington July 26.

As McClellan took over the demoralized army, General Joseph E.
Johnston, who had failed to play Patterson's game in the Shenandoah Valley and had fought at Bull Run, was starting to fortify the
prize that had been won. Redoubts were built around the rail junction at Manassas and artillery was mounted downstream on the Virginia shore, making the water approach to Washington dangerous.
This was not the time for the Federals to move.

Henry Higginson, by now a close friend of Shaw, remembered
years later that one of Shaw's duties in the idle days at Harper's
Ferry was to apprehend runaway slaves and return them to their
masters. Shaw found this duty painful but, as Higginson noted, he
had no choice but to obey his government whose policy toward
slavery, as long as the slaves in question were not actively engaged
in pursuit of the rebellion, was to let it stand.

Before Shaw left Harper's Ferry at the end of July, the luckless General Patterson had been replaced by General Banks. Nathaniel P. Banks was a handsome devil, youngish looking, with bright eyes, a shock of dark hair and a luxuriant mustache. He had served as governor of Massachusetts from 1858 to 1861. He was not a military man, and this would become evident during his checkered war years. He was destined to sail for Louisiana late in 1862 and there, as commander of the Department of the Gulf, would have Negro regiments in his command.

The Second camped on the western face of Maryland Heights, a hoot and a holler from Harper's Ferry, and here Shaw spent many of the idle hours inseparable from a soldier's life. One of his friends was Morris Copeland, the regiment's quartermaster, with whom he and Greely Curtis had ridden out to form a wagon train on that fine spring day in West Roxbury. Shaw liked Copeland and Copeland, no moderate where slavery and arming of blacks were concerned, influenced Shaw, who, at first, seemed no more anxious to arm the Negro than was President Lincoln. On August 6, Shaw wrote, "Mr. Copeland (Quartermaster) told me he had had a long talk with General Banks about making use of the negroes against the Secessionists. I thought it a waste of breath, but we hear today that Banks has offered him a place on his staff, which shows that he thinks a good deal of his opinion. Copeland's sole subject of thought, now, seems to be slavery and he is always fuming and raging about it."

On the same day, Shaw wrote to Sidney Howard Gay, who was serving on the staff of the powerful *New York Daily Tribune* and was a neighbor of the Shaws on Staten Island. Shaw mentioned to Gay the need for greater discipline in some of the regiments in Banks's command and compared the good discipline in the Second with the lack of it in others. It seemed that in boredom and frustration the men of the Fifth Connecticut had recently engaged in a drunken orgy, forcing their officers to call out the officers and noncoms of the Massachusetts Second to help put down the rioting. Shaw was disgusted by the brawling performance, not on moral grounds but because of the weakness of the officers of the Connecticut regiment. There had been many a case of bloodied knuckles and noses, and one of Shaw's sergeants had his arm in a sling.

Then, writing to Gay, Shaw got down to a different kind of

business. He asked Gay an interesting question. "Isn't it extraordinary that the Government won't make use of the instrument that would finish the war sooner than anything else—viz the slaves? I have no doubt they could give more information about the enemy than anyone else, and that there would be nothing easier than to have a line of spies right into their camp. What a lick it would be to them, to call all the blacks in the country to come and enlist in our army! They would probably make a fine army after a little drill, and could certainly be kept under better discipline than our independent Yankees."

To be sure Negroes had supplied Northern commanders with information but Shaw was indulging in a certain amount of fancy where the spying of blacks was concerned and he was oversimplifying the problems involved in enlisting Negroes. He was echoing for the first time the then radical sentiments of Negro leader Frederick Douglass who had written in his *Monthly* that a lenient war would be a lengthy war, that it could be stopped upon the soil where it had originated by " '*carrying the war into Africa.' Let the slaves and free colored people be called into service, and formed into a liberating army* to march into the South and raise the banner of Emancipation among the slaves." Now Shaw was firmly on record and, the antislavery community being what it was, his sentiments would come to the attention of Governor Andrew.

During idle hours on Maryland Heights, perhaps in the quiet of his tent, Shaw thought back to an evening months before when he had taken a girl named Annie Haggerty to the opera in New York. Since that evening, Annie had been much on Shaw's mind. He had known her family, had seen her several times at home, but the evening at the opera had marked a turning point. Shaw's sister Sue and Annie Haggerty were close friends. Shaw, too shy to ask Annie for a photograph, wrote to Susie to send him one. During the genesis of his love for Annie, Susie seems to have been his confidante.

Shaw had missed Bull Run, but he felt the sting of it nonetheless and wanted to fight. So far, he had seen no more than a scurrying Confederate picket. On August 19, he heard for the first time the sound of hostile musketry. A detachment of enemy cavalry entered Harper's Ferry, just across the river, and for a few hours shots rang out, echoing against the surface of the water as members of the Second exchanged rifle fire with Rebel horsemen. Detachments from the Second escorted wagon trains, guarded bridges and fords. In the sprawling camps around Maryland Heights, in sweltering heat and driving rain, the boys of the Second drilled, stood inspection and went out on picket duty.

Shaw liked army life in spite of its hardships and privations. He saw the beauty in things around him—in what to most others were commonplace. He had been stirred by distant glimpses of the Blue Ridge and by the tree-lined gorges of Harper's Ferry, touched by passing images made by men against these wonders. He delighted in the flicker of the cooking fires, the sound of a bugle or the long roll echoing across the hills. He was saddened by a familiar dirge as the lamps in the tents were turned down low. "We are going home," the men sang—as if, with all their hearts, they were trying to believe it.

On August 20, General Banks ordered Shaw's commander, Colonel Gordon, to destroy what food could not be carted off and to take down the telegraph lines in the vicinity of Harper's Ferry. They would move east to join Banks's main body. At Darnestown, the regiment settled down long enough for Shaw to write some letters. He wrote to his sister, Josephine, who was still with the family in West New Brighton. Josephine had a firm place in Shaw's affections and he had always found her an amusing companion. She was highly intelligent and beautifully educated and, like her parents and Shaw himself, had a well-developed social conscience. In October of the following year, Josephine would marry Shaw's friend, Beau Sabreur Charles Russell Lowell, Jr., and hope for a while that the remarkable and attractive Lowell might live to the end of the war. Years later William James would write of her, "She was surely one of the noblest and freest." He would remember Lowell and Josephine as he had seen them on horseback, watching a dress parade of Shaw's Negro regiment. "I looked back and saw their faces against the evening sky, and they looked so young and victorious."

After Lowell died a hero's death at Cedar Creek, Josephine would become a tireless social worker. Now she had lighter things on her mind. She had written Shaw that she was about to start out on a sailing cruise with her sister Nellie, that they planned to put in at Hadley's Harbor at Naushon to visit the family of John Murray

Forbes. Thinking of his visit to Naushon in the spring of '59 and of pleasant times on Staten Island, Shaw wrote Josephine that he often imagined himself "walking about on shady lawns, sitting on piazzas after dinner with a mild cigar, riding or rowing. . . ." He wrote of visions of muslin skirts, jemmy straw hats, white cuffs and collars. Then, getting back to his regiment, he told his sister about the regiment's color bearer. "He was color bearer for a Russian regiment in the Crimea, and was taken prisoner by some English soldiers. When he enlisted in this regiment, he found that one of his captors was in the same company that he was put into! If it is true, it is a more extraordinary coincidence than Mr. Pickwick's being put into prison on St. Valentine's day."

Inactivity gave Shaw a literary turn of mind and he asked his family to send him an edition of Shakespeare's plays published by Phillips and Samson, in which each play was in a separate pamphlet. He said he would like "a few good books of poetry, and some essays, such as Bacon's, Macaulay's and Lamb's. . . ." Several years later, Greely Curtis wrote of his friendship with Shaw, spoke of hours when he and Shaw had read together. Shaw had such a happy disposition that Curtis had found it, "always pleasant to be near him." Curtis had often gone to Shaw's tent to "sit and read, when neither of us would say a word for an hour."

For nearly two months on the hills and in the valleys around Darnestown, along the highways and byways, there were encampments of the regiments of Banks's command. For two months not a hostile shot was heard. Faintly in the distance came the sounds of regimental bands swelling and falling in the evening breeze. At starlight came the notes of tattoo. The Second's sentinels went down to the Potomac in the sultry days and waved to their counterparts across the water, then, growing bolder, they swam the river, shook hands with the Confederates and sat around and talked about home and girls and the coming fighting.

Shaw's days were filled with reveilles, paper work, drills and parades. At mess, there were corncakes, pork and beans, there was bitter coffee and, once in a while, a package came from home—crumbling cookies and dried fruit or, most welcome of all, a box of cigars.

8.

McClellan, the brilliant young man who had had so much so soon, was by now the idol of nearly every soldier in the Army of the Potomac. By mid-October, the morale of his soldiers was as high as it had been since the defeat at Bull Run. McClellan decided to put out a feeler. He would claim no responsibility for the details of the plan or the result, but the reconnaissance-in-force in the direction of Leesburg, though of small military moment, would kill Colonel Edward Baker, a good friend of Lincoln who had served in the Senate, and bring on a chain of Congressional explosions. The blame for the blunder would fall heavily and tragically on Brigadier General Charles P. Stone. As the smoke cleared, McClellan would replace venerable General Winfield Scott as general-in-chief of the entire army.

Shortly after midnight, on October 22, the men of the Second Massachusetts marched briskly off by the light of the moon with high hopes of a good fight. As clouds gathered and blotted out the moon, they marched toward the Potomac to assist a brigade under Colonel Baker, said to be in trouble at Ball's Bluff, just across the river from Conrad's Ferry and thirty miles or so upstream from Washington. They arrived at Conrad's Ferry in a pouring rain, having encountered elements of the Fifteenth Massachusetts along the road. There they discovered that Baker's brigade, including the Fifteenth and Twentieth Massachusetts, had been routed by a superior Confederate force. The Federal soldiers had been ferried to Virginia in an old yawl, a scow and an assortment of rowboats, the river being quite deep and about three quarters of a mile wide at that point. Having been driven back to the river from the vicinity of Leesburg, some had swum or been ferried across to the Maryland side and many more had drowned in the flight. Wounded Yankees, recently ferried back to Maryland, were lying in rows on the sodden ground waiting to be taken to the hospital. Among the wounded, Shaw found Jim Lowell, younger brother of Charles who would

marry Shaw's sister. Lowell was unconscious, having refused surgery
because he knew his wounds would prove fatal. Shaw knelt by the
side of young Oliver Wendell Holmes, Jr. Shaw reported that
Holmes had a ball through his leg and one "through his lungs."[1]
Holmes, of course, recovered from his wounds and in later life became the most prominent Supreme Court justice of his time.

Charles Russell Lowell, Jr. and his sister Anna, who had come
down to visit, were not far from the scene of the debacle and when
they heard that their brother Jim was lying wounded, they rushed
to the scene, but Jim died before they arrived. The morning after
the fight, as had become the custom, a detachment of Yankees
crossed the river under a flag of truce to bury their dead. Having
seen his Massachusetts brothers lying wounded, feeling that the war
was in stalemate if not going badly, Shaw's impatience and boredom
became acute. Summer had passed, fall was wearing on and winter,
by tradition, was a time of inaction. Shaw knew that, for a time at
least, cold and mud would make Virginia an unimportant theater
of war and, feeling that the focus was shifting to the West, he
thought more than once of asking for a transfer to his old idol
Frémont. Shaw's discontent was sharpened by the departure of
Henry Higginson and Greely Curtis to join the First Regiment
of Massachusetts Cavalry. Cavalrymen of Civil War days had all
the glamor of the "wild blue yonder" boys of World War II but,
for some reason, Shaw didn't seek a commission in a cavalry regiment.

On Thanksgiving Day, in camp near Seneca, Maryland, Shaw
and Morse took to the festivities with enthusiasm. The foliage was
blazing. The nip of cold was in the air. After morning services
there was a turkey shoot and a gala dinner. It took twelve hundred
pounds of plum pudding to meet the regiment's needs. Shaw wrote
that the officers' mess tent was lit by dozens of candles, bayonets

---

[1] In Holmes's own account of his experiences at Ball's Bluff, he fails to
mention a wound in his leg. He tells of visits from some of his friends,
among them Norwood Hallowell who would be for a time Shaw's second-
in-command when Shaw was colonel of the Fifty Fourth. Holmes doesn't
mention Shaw's visit but this is not surprising since Holmes tells us that
he was heavily drugged, that his memory of the events at Ball's Bluff was
faulty. As Holmes lay "dying" he characteristically debated with himself
about the meaning of death. His friend Harry Sturgis told Holmes later
that, when he came around and broke into Holmes's thoughts, Holmes
said, "Well Harry I'm dying but I'll be G. d'd if I know where I'm going."

serving as candlesticks. On Christmas Day Shaw sat in his tent
and penned a letter to his family. He wrote soberly of British in-
clination to recognize the Confederacy. "I should be very sorry to
have a war with England. . . . War isn't declared yet, but doesn't
it look very much like it to everyone at home?" He wrote of Christmas Eve, "It began to snow about midnight and I suppose no one
ever had a better chance of seeing 'Santa Claus'; but, as I had my
stockings on, he probably thought it not worth his while to come
down to the guard tent."

Christmas was followed by New Year's Eve and the soldiers in
Maryland didn't let it pass without making hay. Shaw went to an
elaborate ball given by a colonel of the Maryland Home Brigade.
He found the girls pretty, but their dancing didn't please him as
much as their looks. In Shaw's opinion, the best dancer at the ball
was a Jewish girl from Philadelphia who had, much to the dis-
pleasure of her orthodox family, married a gentile captain in a
Massachusetts regiment.

In winter quarters at Frederick, the officers and men were visited
by members of their families and some went north for a glimpse
of home. Shaw's father came down and on another occasion Shaw
had a visit from his sister, Susie, and Annie Haggerty, but during
the visit Shaw lacked the chance or the courage to declare his love
for Annie. Shaw went into Frederick, most often with Charlie Morse,
and wandered the streets of the cold and shabby little town or
stopped at the barbershop for a shave and a haircut, tonics and
unguents.

Shaw found some Marylanders opposed to slavery and others
violently secessionist. One Maryland girl turned up her nose and
made nasty faces whenever she saw a Yankee fighting man. She
made a pointed remark when Shaw was standing near her in the
street. "I like a *nigger* better than a Massachusetts soldier!"

In his history of the regiment, the Second's chaplain Alonzo Quint
noted that intemperance was a problem. He wrote, "Frederick was
filled with liquor shops. General Banks issued an order, on the
10th of February, about 'the alarming increase of intemperance,' and
how 'ill-disposed persons' were selling liquor 'to the detriment and
discredit of the service, the injury of the men, and the danger of
the public;' and he declared it the 'duty of every officer in his command at once to take the most effective measures to suppress this

evil.' Provosts were to shut up certain places and make arrests. Colonel Gordon did take effective measures; so effective, that a liquor-selling Dutchman just across the road came over one day in wrath: 'Your officer come to my house, and did speel my leetel beer.' "

As the New Year wore on, a rift opened between McClellan and the Administration. Some Washington pundits began to whisper that McClellan was a traitor. At best, the man's will to fight was questioned. The previous November when he had been made general-in-chief of all the armies he had accepted the job in a cocksure spirit. Now, looking to spring and under pressure from the Administration, McClellan ordered Banks to move into Virginia.

The Second broke camp and boarded trains for Harper's Ferry. Having crossed the new pontoon bridge, they found that many Harper's Ferry residents had had enough of the town and that there was plenty of sleeping space in empty mold-smelling houses. The following morning, February 28, the regiment moved out to Charlestown where John Brown had been tried and hanged. Shaw described it as a "wretched hole." The regiment entered town amid a shower of chicken feathers. Shaw, describing the foraging, wrote that the Second Massachusetts and several other regiments were "attacked by a large body of pigs, turkeys, chickens and ducks . . . and as some of these Secessionist animals met their death in the fray, it was no sin to eat them."

As the feathers settled, General McClellan appeared. The regiment's chaplain wrote that McClellan won the hearts of the men. He seemed not to notice the aftermath of the battle of the barnyard and took the cheers of the men with his usual grace.

The Second took up residence in the courthouse where John Brown had been tried and sentenced. The windows of the regiment's temporary quarters looked diagonally across to the two-story jail where Brown had been imprisoned. The night was cold and Shaw was glad to have a roof over his head. Shaw and a handful of his fellow officers were quartered in the office of the Honorable Andrew Hunter, the prosecuting attorney at Brown's trial. Shaw wrote, "I am using his pen, ink and paper."

The officers found a rich crop of records in Hunter's office and Shaw was fascinated with the material. There were piles of papers and memoranda about the trial, testimony and confessions of members of Brown's company. Shaw saw letters from Virginia's Governor Wise, President Buchanan and Lydia Maria Child, a lifelong friend of Shaw's mother. There were letters from people in all parts of the country, some writers interceding for Brown, some "hoping and praying that he would be executed without delay."

Shaw commented that an anonymous correspondent in New York had said that Thomas Wentworth Higginson had been a principal in the plot. Dr. Higginson, pastor of the Free Church of Worcester, Massachusetts, was an Abolitionist of radical stripe and a well-known Boston man of letters. He had made no secret of his support of John Brown and had long hurled insults at slave states and slavery in general. He had supported Brown with money and suggestions. Incidentally, other prominent Abolitionists who had given visible support to Brown didn't think that in any state in the Union they would be safe from the long arm of Federal law. Frederick Douglass, Franklin B. Sandborn, George L. Stearns and Dr. Samuel G. Howe had fled to Canada after Brown's capture. Higginson had listened to Lysander Spooner's wildly romantic plot to obtain Brown's freedom by kidnaping Governor Wise, but the plan had foundered when the plotters failed to raise enough money to buy a tug for the purpose of steaming up the James River to corral the Governor. After Brown's execution, Higginson still had had high hopes of freeing Albert Hazlit and handsome lady-killing Aaron Stevens, two of Brown's men who had still been alive in the Charlestown jail. Higginson had traveled to Harrisburg to meet Kansas jayhawker James Montgomery and plan a rescue. Montgomery had gone down to Charlestown with a clowning, play-acting man named Silas Soulé to look things over. Montgomery had been born in Kentucky and his soft Southern manners and Soulé's affected Irish accent and drunken gait had fooled the militia that swarmed over Charlestown, but the plotters had finally been discouraged, not only by the difficulties of the operation, but by the captives themselves who were not in favor of more bloodletting in hopeless plots.

In Hunter's desk, Shaw also found a great many notes for sermons which had been delivered in "Kansas, Iowa, & c., . . ." Shaw concluded his discussion of the papers. "It may seem to some that we should not have touched Mr. Hunter's papers, but I don't think there is anything wrong in it. He is in the Virginia Secessionist Legislature and was one of the early Rebels."

Shortly after Shaw's stay in Charlestown, Thomas Wentworth Higginson would go to Port Royal to take command of the First South Carolina Volunteers, a Negro regiment, and James Montgomery would follow Higginson to Port Royal to organize the Second South Carolina Volunteers, also a Negro regiment. Shaw and his Fifty-Fourth Massachusetts Regiment would, for a time, be brigaded under Montgomery, and for Shaw it would be a painful and frustrating experience.

In mid-March McClellan lost his job as general-in-chief of all the armies but retained nominal command of the Army of the Potomac. Colonel Gordon, as part of Banks's corps, was ordered to march to Winchester where a large Federal force was rumored to be in serious trouble with Stonewall Jackson. This, in fact, was not the case, but the rumor was a forecast of things to come. Federal forces in the Shenandoah Valley would have little but trouble with General Jackson until Robert E. Lee would order him east in the middle of June.

Across the state in eastern Virginia the Peninsular campaign would soon begin, and McClellan, even now, was moving men and equipment to Alexandria for embarkation to Hampton Roads. By the end of the month, 75,000 soldiers and a variety of equipment, including a brace of observation balloons, would be in the vicinity of Fortress Monroe making ready to advance on Richmond. It was an impressive movement but McClellan, who had so recently lost his job as general-in-chief of the entire army, had not found it easy to persuade the Administration to fall in with his plans. McClellan's campaign was destined to become a signal failure, and while it was in progress he would show unmistakable signs of the lack of pugnacity that would eventually lead to his removal.

Shaw wrote of the march to Winchester, "The weather was fine and we had bright moonlight all the way. I never saw anything more picturesque than some of our bivouacks in the groves on this road. The trees are very fine and look beautiful in the moonlight with the smoke of forty or fifty fires curling among them. An artist would find many opportunities for his pencil."

While the men rested, the rumor came that "Jackson had marched to the rear of our force at Winchester and captured seven thousand men." The battle was reportedly still in progress and Shaw, sensing a chance to fight at last, marched south in high spirits. There were spontaneous cheers along the route of march and the chaplain wrote that the men enlivened the road with the strains of "Dixie."

The rescuers reached Winchester, which Shaw described as a "tumbledown place, with some good houses, and a great many trees" and found that there had been no battle at all. The wily Jackson had disappeared behind the hills. General Banks was ordered to move east across the Blue Ridge, leaving General Shields to garrison the town. As soon as Gordon's brigade reached the mountain pass, Jackson came out of hiding to drive off what he thought was a token force. He met Shields at Kernstown, three miles south of Winchester and, as the cannon sounded, Gordon turned back to help subdue Jackson. By the time Gordon's men arrived on the scene, the battle was over. Shaw found Winchester full of "prisoners and wounded of both armies." The majority of the wounded, Shaw found, had been left "on bare floors of the hotels and public buildings without even straw to lie upon." He found about twenty dead men laid out in the entry of the courthouse with the capes of their overcoats over their faces.

Jackson had been driven off and, as Banks's corps took off in pursuit, it was led by the Second. Shaw and his men put out fires under heavy wooden bridges, moved forward through driving rain. After the rain, Shaw was aware of the smell of green winter wheat by the side of the road and the dipping flight of a frightened swallow. At one settlement, country folk gathered to gape at the instruments of the regimental band. One woman, more innocent than the others, was roundly teased into believing that the tuba was an instrument of war. A bandsman told her it was called a "bell-teaser" and was "terribly destructive at short distances."

During the weeks that followed, as Jackson played cat and mouse with Banks there were frequent artillery brawls and some picket stalking. Pot shots were taken at Jackson's ghostly marauders under dashing cavalry genius Turner Ashby who drew the Yankees south.

Shaw, sick and tired of punching at shadows, longed for solid contact with his enemy and dreamed of taking part in the destruction of Jackson. Early in May, he wrote of a midnight march across the Massanutten Range to engage a phantom force which was said to be threatening General Sullivan. Reaching a pinnacle just at dawn, Shaw thought the sight worth the trouble of the march. "We could see for miles and miles down both valleys East and West.

The sun was shining brightly in one, and the other was grey, excepting the peaks of the distant mountains; I never saw anything so beautiful."

General Sullivan was astonished at the appearance of his saviors and said he hadn't seen so much as an enemy courier.

In May, Stanton directed that Banks's corps be split, some regiments to return to Strasburg and others to move east to Fredricksburg. The Second Massachusetts made for Strasburg.

On March 13, under the sponsorship of New England antislavery forces, an act had passed Congress which would point the way to more definitive moves on the part of the "radical" Republicans. "All officers or persons in the military or naval service of the United States are prohibited from employing any of the forces under their respective commands for the purpose of returning fugitives from service or labor, who may have escaped from any persons to whom such service or labor is claimed to be due, and any officer who shall be found guilty by a court-martial of violating this article shall be dismissed from the service."

Officers of Massachusetts regiments needed little encouragement. As the Second marched to Strasburg, it was accompanied by an undernourished slave and her child. The slave, Peggy, had been treated badly by her widowed mistress and was taken on as an assistant cook. She would stay with the regiment until she could be sent north to Massachusetts.

During May, Shaw, for the first time, seriously considered serving as an officer in a Negro regiment. On May 19, he wrote his father, "You will be surprised to see that I am in Washington. I came down with Major Copeland to see if I could assist him at all, in a plan he has made for getting up a black regiment. He says, very justly, that it would be much wiser to enlist men in the North, who have had the courage to run away, and have already suffered for their freedom, than to take them all from contrabands at Port Royal and other places. . . . Copeland wants me to take hold of the black regiment with him, if he can get permission to raise it, and offers me a major's commission in it." Shaw concluded, "Copeland thinks that the raising of black regiments will be the greatest thing that has ever been done for the negro race."

Within a short time, Copeland was to have a difference with the Administration over quite another matter and would be dismissed from the service under tragic conditions,[2] but, like Shaw's earlier interest in expanded Negro participation in the war, his interest in Copeland's project would not be overlooked.

From Washington, Shaw went to Staten Island for a brief visit, leaving for Winchester on May 23 to rejoin his regiment. His family stood on the porch and waved good-by as he walked down the path. Later, Shaw wrote that the visit seemed like a dream.

As Shaw returned to the Shenandoah Valley, Jackson was launching what would turn out to be a brilliant campaign against Banks, a campaign in which the hapless Banks would be deceived and harassed unmercifully and driven back across the Potomac. Banks's force, which had been nearly twice as large as Jackson's, had been reduced and Jackson's strengthened. Banks was to have summered at Strasburg, eighteen miles south of Winchester, but Jackson had other plans for him. By the end of April, Shaw had lost patience with his commander. "There is no doubt that an enterprising man might have taken General Banks and his staff in their beds more than once since we left Harper's Ferry." He complained, "My faith has given out at last—a good many others lost theirs last summer. I don't believe we shall ever have a chance to do anything."

Banks was at Strasburg as Jackson moved in from the east, driving toward Winchester. Banks ordered a retreat. As his slow-moving columns of wagons and men lumbered along the Valley Pike, Jackson's advance knifed forward, his men pushed to the limit of their endurance, their commander hoping to finish Banks off once and

---

[2] Copeland was dismissed from the army in August of 1862 after the retreat of the Union forces from Winchester, Virginia. Considering his performance in past "fights" it is safe to assume that, because he was by chance in Boston at the time of the engagement and retreat, he was in an agony of frustration at being absent from the scene of action. The retreat, before General Jackson, occasioned alarm in the North, and Governor Andrew again called on available Massachusetts men to rush to the defense of Washington. Andrew's appeal was followed by an appeal published in the *Boston Daily Advertiser* on May 26, 1862, and signed by Morris R. Copeland who was then Banks's adjutant general. Copeland's appeal was in fiery prose and called on the civilians of Massachusetts to "seize the musket and sabre!" Copeland was imprudent. He blamed Stanton for the retreat in Virginia. Tragic as Copeland's dismissal was, available evidence indicates that the Administration was justified in dismissing a man who publicly blamed his superiors for a retreat. After his dismissal, Copeland sought an interview with Lincoln who, when he saw Copeland, seems to have had little patience with his appeal.

for all. As Shaw traveled south, his regiment fought off elements of Jackson's force. A halt was ordered at Kernstown and the wounded gathered into one of the houses. Jackson pressed his attack, and the retreat continued to the fringes of Winchester where a defensive line was drawn. Here, as the day ended, Shaw found his company and was sent out on patrol. The sporadic fire of skirmishers sounded through the night, and in the early hours of May 25, the Yankee outposts were driven in and a battle began. As daylight came on, the Federal line broke and Banks's forces fell back from the heights and retreated along the main street of the town, harassed all the way by Confederate soldiers who shot at them from alleys and parallel streets. To add to the difficulty of retreat, Winchester civilians hied themselves to the windows and doors of their tumble-down houses and fired on the Yankees. Old men and women leveled smoothbores at the soldiers from upstairs windows, younger women fired pistols from open doorways. Here Shaw's company commander, Captain Mudge, was wounded in street fighting and Shaw's life was saved by his gold watch which turned aside a rifle bullet. "The ball would undoubtedly have entered my stomach, and as it was, bruised my hip a good deal. The watch was in the pocket of my vest, though I almost always carry it in my fob. I felt a violent blow and a burning sensation in my side, and at the same moment a man by my side cried out, 'O my arm!'" Shaw wrote, "You don't know how queerly the bullets sound whistling about your head. It seems as if you must surely be hit."

Shaw reported that, in his company of fifty, one was killed, eight wounded and two taken prisoner in the retreat. Banks's force as a whole was badly cut up, and he had had to bring all his resources to bear to keep the retreat from becoming a rout.

Several months after the fight at Winchester, Shaw was delighted to learn that a sergeant who had fought near him on the eve of the retreat and in Winchester streets thought that Shaw had shown courage and coolness throughout this first tilt with enemy troops.

The Second formed the rear of the column in a thirty-two-mile retreat along the Shenandoah Valley on the Martinsburg road. At Martinsburg, the retreat halted as Jackson turned aside and hard-tack was given to the hungry soldiers. Banks's forces recrossed the Potomac and Shaw's regiment went into camp up the river at Williamsport. Here, in letters to his family, he expressed anxiety at reports of barbaric treatment of prisoners of war by the enemy. He was especially concerned about brave and popular Major Wilder Dwight, but after Dwight was exchanged and returned to the regiment, he dispelled such reports. Jackson, it seems, had treated the captured, especially the wounded, with extraordinary kindness.

Banks's corps crossed back into Virginia on June 10 and, once again, made for Winchester where they passed through the town in close order, with drums beating time, to prevent the men from breaking ranks and taking vengeance on the self-styled guerrillas that lurked in the houses. The corps crossed the Blue Ridge at Front Royal and became part of the command of blustering, bragging General John Pope.

Gordon, who had been a colonel in the Massachusetts Second, was a general now and commanded the brigade to which the Second belonged. In July Shaw was offered a place on Gordon's staff, and since nothing much was happening he found the change welcome. He soon found that, though he had more freedom and could sleep later in the mornings, the duties of an aide-de-camp were more like those of an orderly than the duties of a soldier. He bought a "nice little mare," took pleasant rides through the countryside and wrote a great many letters full of small talk and reminiscence. He reported the news of the death of one of his men who had been hit during the retreat through Winchester's streets and had been carried north in an ambulance. "He was badly wounded in the thigh, but I had no idea he would die when I last saw him. The bone was shattered and the doctor said his constitution couldn't bear the drain. He didn't expect to die, and as he lay on the bed, he had the sweetest and most patient expression on his face you can imagine."

Shaw wrote that he had seen the colorful and much-talked-of teen-age siren Belle Boyd. She had given "Fred d'Hauteville a very pretty Secession flag, which she said she carried when she went out to meet Jackson's troops coming into Front Royal." Belle Boyd would be imprisoned and released a number of times before the end of the war. When she had met Jackson near Front Royal she had given him valuable information about the disposition of Federal troops. Shaw and his friends, as did most Yankees who met this young charmer, doubted very much that she was a spy.

Some Virginians were friendly without design. On the way to Washington in May, Shaw and Copeland had been befriended by a Virginia family. Now Shaw wrote that he had visited them again. "I got there about an hour after tea, and they insisted on getting up a second meal for me. Of course I said I hoped they wouldn't, which was a great lie, as I was very hungry. They saw through it and fed me to my heart's content on honey, bread and butter, apple sauce, and tea; one of the young ladies sitting near, meanwhile, brushing away the flies with a broom made of peacock's feathers."

In answer to some questions of his mother about Negro enlistment in the Federal army, Shaw wrote optimistically about integration, which wasn't finally achieved in the United States Army until the war in Korea. "About having negroes in our present white regiments, I think the men would object to it very strongly at first, but they would get accustomed to it in time."

In August, as the second Bull Run campaign took shape, Shaw saw action for the second time. General Pope was moving toward Richmond along the Orange and Alexandria Railroad, and Lee detached Jackson from the lines around Richmond where McClellan was about to withdraw from the peninsula. Lee sent Jackson north to "suppress" Pope.

South of Culpepper and three or four miles west of the Rapidan River, a hill called Cedar Mountain rose out of a plain. Here Banks, commanding two undersized divisions, was surprised again by his nemesis, Jackson. Here a battle was fought in which Jackson was at first thrown off balance, then swept the field driving Banks before him. Gordon's brigade, having been originally designated as reserve, plunged forward to fill a gap in the Union line and was driven back. As the tide turned against them, quite a few men were captured, among them Harry Russell who, with Shaw, had been called to the side of their dying grandfather when they were boys. While they were both in the Second their friendship had deepened. Shaw, who was bringing up artillery as his regiment was beaten back, moved through a little wood toward the sound of musketry and as he emerged he "saw the last of Harry. I was about opposite to his company a few paces in the rear, and he called out, 'Hullo Bob!' and came to where I was. We talked a few minutes together about what was going on, and then he went back to his place and stood, pulling his moustache and looking over the field, the bullets whistling thick around him. He was perfectly quiet but he looked pretty fierce."

The battle was reckoned as a victory for Jackson but it accomplished little. This was simply the start of a series of moves by Lee which would force Pope's retreat to the upper Rappahannock where Lee would confuse and crush Pope at the second battle of Bull Run.

After the battle, finding Pope's main force not far away, Jackson withdrew behind the Rapidan and, after his withdrawal, Shaw went over the field with General Gordon. He found five of his friends who had fallen in battle. He mentioned respected and capable Richard Cary who, with his wife, had lived in Mobile and New Orleans before the war but had come north to join the army as the war had begun. Shaw wrote of the five, "Oh! it is hard to believe we will never see them again." The first man Shaw recognized was Cary. "He was lying on his back with his head on a piece of wood. He looked calm and peaceful as if he were merely sleeping; his face was beautiful, and I could have stood and looked at it a long while."

After Cedar Mountain, the Second, still under Pope, would form part of his extreme right while Second Bull Run was being fought. They would take no part in the disastrous engagement.

9.

Events near Sharpsburg, Maryland, and a Presidential proclamation would mark a great turning point in the history of his country and in Shaw's life.

The afternoon of September 15 found Shaw's regiment near meandering Antietam Creek which wound through pretty, rolling country, patches of woodland, pastures and wheat fields and fields of tasseled corn, past an occasional whitewashed house or unpainted barn.

Since Second Bull Run, great changes had been made in the Army of the Potomac. McClellan's power had been slowly siphoned off by the Administration, but now, to reorganize the army after defeat, Lincoln had restored McClellan to favor. Lincoln, whose faith in McClellan as a commander in the field had been badly shaken, saw that he was still an enormously popular man who could restore to the soldiers their sense of pride. To be sure, McClellan's character had undergone no startling change. He thought the capital might be saved but he wasn't taking any chances. Early in September he had seen to it that his wife's silver was sent away to a safer place. But McClellan was loved by the men and he was a capable organizer. For a time, at least, he was the man for the job.

On September 5, Lee had crossed the Potomac into western Maryland hoping to defeat McClellan's army. Lee had his reasons for challenging an army twice as big as his own. Like the good general he was, he wanted to retain the initiative and there was still a chance that he might spark a revolt in Maryland. Perhaps more important than either of these was the hope that any measure of military success just now would bring foreign recognition to the Confederate government. So Lee moved north, keeping South Mountain between himself and his enemy.

Until McClellan knew exactly where Lee could be found, he had dared not leave Washington undefended. But it had been clear that Lee must be engaged and defeated—at least driven off, or the

Northern cause, in deep trouble now, would be lost beyond recall. Even in the West, where things had looked promising not long ago, the Union had lost the initiative. Never again would the Confederacy's lamp burn as brightly as it was burning now. The British, long in sympathy with the South, could see the dissolution of Northern hopes of bringing the war to a swift conclusion. On Christmas Day of the previous year, Shaw had expressed anxiety at the prospect of war with England. Now it was apparent to everyone including Shaw that the opening shot of a war with England would be the crack of doom. And now it looked very much to British statesmen as if the North was on the brink of disaster. A London *Times* dispatch, filed in New York on September 16, would say in part, "amid many shiftings and twistings of fortune, nothing has been so evident to all men as the ultimate hopelessness of the Northern project."

As McClellan had stirred himself to seek out Lee, a document had fallen into his hands, a document that should have enabled him to destroy Lee's army of northern Virginia before the turning of the autumn leaves. One of Lee's officers had lost a copy of Lee's campaign orders and these had been found by a Federal soldier wrapped neatly around three cigars. With Lee's orders in hand, McClellan had moved out to meet Lee. Now the stage was set for the inevitable battle.

Now, on the fifteenth, Shaw's regiment was part of McClellan's army, facing the ragged and tough but outnumbered Confederates across Antietam Creek. This morning, white-whiskered old-timer General Mansfield had replaced General Banks as commander of the Twelfth Corps, the corps to which the Second belonged, and they had moved west across South Mountain through Turner's Gap on the National Road. Turner's Gap and Crampton's Gap, six miles to the south, had been secured the day before and, characteristically, McClellan had failed to move straight through as the gaps had been captured. He had waited through the night. Now, facing his enemy, he waited again until everything was put in apple-pie order, while Lee's reinforcements were moving north.

On the morning of the sixteenth, the landscape was veiled by a thin mist and, even as it burned away, McClellan was silent, still pussyfooting, content with the cheers that greeted him as he rode about behind the lines. The Second's chaplain, Alonzo Quint, remembered the men's reaction when "suddenly McClellan appeared. As the column moved to the side of the road, caps flew in the air, and shouts and cheers rolled up as from one man. They believed in McClellan." And it was on this day that Jackson joined Lee after capturing the garrison at Harper's Ferry, 11,000 prisoners and some supplies.

The lines were forming roughly north and south, the Federal army looking west, making a crescent with Hooker on the right, Mansfield, Sumner and Porter facing the town of Sharpsburg and Burnside on the left, southeast of town. At ten o'clock that night, word reached the Second that Mansfield's corps would march at once to support Hooker who had deployed his corps beyond the creek. Hooker's men had encountered some Rebels but the evening's action amounted to nothing. When things settled down, Shaw rode over to talk to friend and cavalryman Will Forbes[1] who had bivouacked nearby. Shaw and Forbes lay on a blanket by Forbes's fire and Shaw read aloud letters from his sisters Josephine and Nellie, both written on Naushon. At 1 A.M. on the morning of the seventeenth, Shaw rode back to his company and rested in a wheat field with Charlie Morse. The two men slept fitfully, in a drizzling rain, to the tune of constant picket firing until dawn when they were awakened by the awesome thudding of Hooker's fieldpieces as they leveled a cornfield in front of the Dunker church where there were solid lines of Jackson's men and where some bitter fighting was destined to take place. Shaw and Morse scurried around in the misty light, rounding up their men for the coming action. Going through the cornfield, Hooker's men had moved up to the church and were just about to break through Jackson's lines when Rebel reinforcements charged in, yelping like beagles, and Hooker's soldiers were forced to retire, with the enemy close on their heels.

During the fight at the church, Shaw's men had moved forward to a little orchard which was bounded by a rail fence. As Hooker's men retired, Shaw found himself on the flank of the counterattacking foe and, under orders from Colonel Andrews, who with General Gordon had organized the regiment at Brook Farm, directed a cross

---

[1] William Forbes, son of John Murray Forbes.

fire on the enemy's line which, "we soon discovered, did a great deal of execution, and saved the Third Wisconsin from being completely used up. It was the prettiest thing we have ever done, and our loss was small. . . ."

Now the counterattack had been blunted and stalled and it was the enemy's turn to retire. Now Mansfield's corps moved forward through the cornfield, driving Rebels before them, until it finally lost momentum and halted close to the Dunker church. In an open field, beyond the cornfield, Shaw encountered the horrors of modern war; "such a mass of dead and wounded men, mostly Rebels . . . I never saw before; it was a terrible sight, and our men had to be very careful to avoid treading on them; many were mangled and torn to pieces by artillery, but most of them had been wounded by musketry fire. We halted right among them and the men did everything they could for their comfort, giving them water from their canteens and trying to place them in easy positions. There are so many young boys and old men among the Rebels, that it hardly seems possible that they have come out on their own accord to fight us, and it makes you pity them all the more, as they lie moaning on the field. We heard about this time that General Mansfield was mortally wounded. He has been with us only three days but everyone liked him; he took more personal interest in the comfort and welfare of the men than any commander the corps has had. . . .

"The wounded Rebels were always surprised and grateful as men could be at receiving attention from us, and many said that all they wanted was to get to our hospitals, and wished they had never fired a shot at us. One boy seventeen, told Morse he had only left North Carolina three weeks ago and how his father and mother grieved at his going."

While Shaw and his men worked in the field, "Sumner's whole corps swept across, close by us, and advanced into a wood. . . . It was a grand sight. . . ." To Shaw, the mass of charging men looked invincible, but Sumner, like Hooker, was driven back. In fact, Sumner had used a division at a time and his method of attack characterized Federal action that day. First it had been Hooker, then Mansfield, now Sumner and so on down the line, making the day a series of battles instead of one crushing blow that could have shattered Lee's line. McClellan's tactics, if tactics they were, would make it a battle in which neither side would gain a tactical triumph.

History would treat McClellan harshly. A hundred years after Antietam, an historian writing at West Point, where a statue of McClellan stands above the Hudson River, would record a judgment of the general's leadership at Sharpsburg. "On the several occasions when opportunity for a decisive assault had arisen, McClellan had refused to act. Throughout the battle he had neither led nor inspired, but remained little more than a spectator."

Even Shaw, who like most of the soldiers was loyal to McClellan, summed up the day as less than successful. "The result of the battle was, that we remained in possession of the field, and the enemy drew off undisturbed. Whether that is all we wanted I don't know; but I should think not."

Lee's army had been anything but "undisturbed." A blushing triumph had been pulled from the fire. The army of northern Virginia had been hurt badly and it would have to be rebuilt before it could menace the Federals again, but McClellan didn't know the extent of the damage. His intelligence reports were grossly misleading. He had consistently overrated Confederate strength and he did so now. Instead of following Lee across the Potomac, he sat on his hands. When McClellan did move, he would move again with indecision and, eventually, Lincoln would run out of patience and McClellan would lose his command.

Captain Shaw came away from the bloodiest day of the Civil War with no more than a bruise on his neck where he had been struck by a spent ball. His company had been lightly hit. He reported one killed and five wounded. Caspar Crowninshield, the football star of Shaw's freshman year at Harvard, was wounded for the second time, but Crowninshield would survive the war. Shaw wrote of a less fortunate friend, handsome, soft-eyed Major Wilder Dwight, "I suppose you know that poor Dwight is dead; he was very anxious to live until his Father and Mother could get here. He is a great loss to us as well as to them; it will be a terrible blow to his Mother as he was her favorite son. . . ."

On the evening of the seventeenth, when the tumult had died, Shaw and Charlie Morse surveyed the scene. "At last night came on, and, with the exception of an occasional shot from the outposts, all was quiet. The crickets chirped, and the frogs croaked, just as if nothing had happened all day long, and presently the stars came out bright, and we lay down among the dead and slept soundly until daylight."

In Lee's withdrawal Lincoln saw a chance he had been looking for. On September 22, he presented to his cabinet the preliminary Proclamation of Emancipation which announced that on January 1 of the new year all slaves in states in rebellion against the Union would be free. He presented it modestly but with the confidence of a man who believed that he was the instrument of God's will. Lincoln had seized the initiative at last. At last it seemed that the freedom fought for in the American Revolution might become a reality for all the people. The war which was tearing America apart would become total war as a key question was clearly defined—a question which, for England, had been settled before the American Revolution when Lord Mansfield, in 1773 in the Sommersett case, had said, "The state of slavery is of such a nature, that it is incapable of being introduced on any reasons, moral or political, but only by positive law, which preserves its force long after the reasons, occasion, and time itself from whence it was created, is erased from memory. It is so odious that nothing can be suffered to support it, but positive law. Whatever inconveniences, therefore, may follow from the decision, I cannot say this case is allowed or approved by the law of England; therefore the black must be discharged."

Now perhaps in America, if the Federal armies were victorious, the brandings, whippings and burnings and the splitting of families would come to an end.

In the North, in some quarters, the Proclamation was greeted coolly, though most Negroes and the members of the antislavery community hailed it in jubilation. Ralph Waldo Emerson was one of those who saw it as a profoundly important, far-reaching pronouncement. He wrote, "It is by no means necessary that this measure should be suddenly marked by any signal results on the Negroes or the Rebel masters. The force of the act is that it commits the country to this justice. . . . It is not a measure that admits of being taken back. Done it cannot be undone. . . .

"The same act makes clear that the lives of our heroes have not been sacrificed in vain. It makes a victory of our defeats. Our hurts are healed. The health of the nation is repaired."

Many Northerners decried the issuance of the Proclamation on the grounds that, in their anger, the Southern leaders would toss to the four winds the rules of war. Indeed, in the South, extreme retaliatory measures were proposed, but except in the case of Negro soldiers and their white officers none would be written into law. The South's terror of black soldiers would be spelled out the following year, after Shaw took command of the Fifty-Fourth.

England, intolerant of slavery on her own soil, didn't disapprove it in her former colonies. She needed cotton and her lathes turned out arms for the Rebel government. Plenty of runners slipped through the Federal blockade. News of Lincoln's Proclamation was greeted with derision by members of the British governing class. The London *Times* printed prose that might have been written in Richmond, Virginia. It said that the villainous Lincoln would "whisper of the pleasures of the spoil and of the gratification of yet fiercer instincts; and when blood begins to flow and when shrieks come piercing through the darkness, Mr. Lincoln will wait amid the rising flames, till all is consummated, and then he will rub his hands and think that revenge is sweet. . . ."

But in spite of the reaction of the ruling class and the howlings of the conservative *Times*, the Confederacy's hour of hope for recognition in Europe had passed with Antietam. It was now clear that to side with the South after issuance of Lincoln's Proclamation would be to condone that peculiar institution outlawed in England and frowned on by members of her working class.

Shaw's feelings about the Proclamation were typical, not of anti-slavery sentiment, but of the sentiments of the men in the field, men too close to the stench of war to approve what they believed might bring a descent of unbridled barbarism. On September 25, from Maryland Heights, he wrote, "So the 'Proclamation of Emancipation, has come at last, or rather its forerunner. I suppose you are all very much excited about it. For my part, I can't see what *Practical* good it can do now. Wherever our army has been there remain no slaves, and the Proclamation will not free them where we don't go."

Then Shaw voiced a common fear. "Jeff Davis will soon issue a proclamation threatening to hang every prisoner they take, and will make this a war of extermination."

Shaw was thinking especially of his cousin and devoted friend

Harry Russell, now in Libby Prison. Shaw felt that issuance of the Proclamation was without question, "the right thing to do" but believed that, as a measure taken before the end of the war, its evil consequences would outbalance the good. He was clearly troubled by indecision. He wrote his mother to ask Sidney Howard Gay or George Curtis, both firmly on Lincoln's side, to write him their reasons for favoring the move.

When the jubilation and derisive shouts had died, for Shaw and for everyone else, one fact would stand like an obelisk on a flat plain: slavery was on the line.

After Antietam, Shaw wrote, "I never felt, before, the excitement which makes a man want to rush into the fight, but I did that day. Every battle makes me wish more and more that the war was over. It seems as if nothing could justify a battle like that of the 17th, and the horrors inseparable from it." At the end of the day, Shaw had longed for peace. "The night of the battle, Charlie Morse and I lay together, and talked about our homes, and those of the thousands of dead about; and it seemed to me as if I could see the house and all of you there. If this had been the last battle, what a blessing it would be."

Early in October, Shaw was offered a place on the staff of his former tutor, Frank Barlow, who had just been commissioned brigadier general. Shaw liked and admired Barlow, but he preferred to command his own company and he declined the offer. With the other soldiers of the Army of the Potomac, he settled down for a dreary winter of paper work and domestic chores, drilling his company when it was dry enough, warming himself by cooking fires and, once in a while, taking a week or so of leave. Log huts sprouted on Maryland Heights as camps across the countryside took on an almost permanent air. Furloughs, of course, were occasional bright spots in the muddy landscape of military life. Shaw went north for the wedding of his sister, Susie, a fine occasion with none of the poignant overtones of so many wartime marriages. The bridegroom, Robert Minturn, was a civilian. Shaw found the white tablecloths, the heated rooms and rustling gowns part of a barely believable, bygone world.

On the way back to camp at Maryland Heights, Shaw took time out for a respite from travel, with friends in Frederick. At their house he "heard some beautiful singing by two young ladies, (which didn't set me back any) and had a good tea; after which I embarked, at 7½ P.M., in the cars for Harper's Ferry. I fell asleep and instead of getting out at 'Sandy Hook,' was carried over the river, and had to stumble my weary way, with bag and overcoat, across the pontoon bridge, in the dark to the Maryland side. Just as I was gathering my remaining strength to climb the hill, which was an angle of about 55° with the plain, I ran against a sentinel.

" 'Is Gordon's brigade up there?' says I.

" 'No,' says he.

" 'Where is it?'

" 'I don't know.'

" 'When did it move?'

" 'Four days ago.'

" 'In which direction?'

" 'I don't know.' "

Shaw stumbled back across the swirling, black river and found a provost marshal who declared that the sentinel was an ass. "O, they're all up on Maryland Heights."

At this, Shaw spread his overcoat on the floor, lay down and munched an apple, a farewell gift of his friends in Frederick. The following morning, Shaw struggled up the hill to Maryland Heights and found "nix." But one of the Second Regiment's "hospital men" was up there packing stores and directed Shaw to Gordon's new camp near Sharpsburg.

While in camp at Sharpsburg, Shaw proposed to Annie Haggerty by mail. Her answer[2] was equivocal but she did not refuse him. "I have Annie's answer at last. I feel, after reading her note, that it will come all right in the end."

Gordon's brigade left Sharpsburg on December 10, crossed the Potomac and marched to Stafford Courthouse, Virginia, where they camped near a pine wood. While Shaw was there, it was as cold as the lower reaches of hell, and at night the men slept in their overcoats and bundled in good New England style. After Christmas, Shaw wrote his mother, "The letter you wrote from New York

---

[2] Shortly after Shaw and Annie Haggerty started a regular correspondence, Annie asked Shaw to burn all her letters. Shaw did this, though with much regret. In accordance with her wishes, he probably burned all the letters she wrote him until his death.

reached me on Christmas day, as you thought it might, and that was the only merry thing that happened to me." But there had been a modicum of merriment provided by "a dinner of oysters, chickens, and potatoes, eaten off a clothing box for a table; and after dinner some rum punch."

Shaw was encouraged in his amours when Annie sent him a fine vignette of herself to carry in the breast pocket of his uniform blouse. After Christmas, Shaw went to Lenox, Massachusetts, to visit Annie who was with her mother at the Haggerty farm. There they spoke, for the first time, of their love for each other and Annie promised herself to Shaw. When Shaw left her to go back to camp, he traveled in the evening to Hudson, New York, where he caught a milk train that carried him along the starlit Hudson to New York City. He arrived at Susie's and Bob Minturn's house on lower Fifth Avenue just before dawn and rang the bell over and over but couldn't raise a soul. He sat on the doorstep for more than an hour, watching the sky grow light and listening to the lonely clop of horseshoes on the cobblestones and the creak and rattle of milk wagons making their rounds.

Shaw met Charlie Morse, also on leave, and the two men went back to Stafford Courthouse together. Back in camp, Shaw wrote Annie, "I have thought a great deal of you—indeed almost all the time since I left Lenox—and of my visit to you, especially the last part of it. O, dear! you don't know how much I should like to see you again!"

10.

As we have seen, on February 2, Shaw's father received a letter from Governor Andrew, offering his son the colonelcy of the Fifty-Fourth Massachusetts Regiment which was to be the first Negro regiment raised in the free states of the Northeast. Enclosed in Andrew's letter to Francis Shaw was a letter to the younger Shaw. It was short and to the point:

> Commonwealth of Massachusetts
> Executive Department, Boston
> January 30, 1863.

Captain Robert G. Shaw
2nd Reg. Mass. Vol. Inf.
Captain,
   I am about to organize in Massachusetts a Colored Regiment as part of the volunteer quota of this State—the commissioned officers to be white men. I have today written your Father expressing to him my sense of the importance of this undertaking, and requesting him to forward to you this letter, in which I offer to you the Commission of Colonel over it. The Lieutenant Colonelcy I have offered to Captain Hallowell of the Twentieth Massachusetts Regiment. It is important to the organization of this regiment that I should receive your reply to this offer at the earliest day consistent with your ability to arrive at a deliberate conclusion on the subject.

> Respectfully and very truly yours,
> JOHN A. ANDREW
> *Governor of Massachusetts.*

Norwood Hallowell, born in Philadelphia, was the son of a prominent and wealthy Quaker gentleman. Hallowell accepted Andrew's offer without hesitation and went to Boston as soon as his papers were in order.[1]

Shaw's father decided to leave that night for his son's camp at

---

[1] On May 30, 1863, Norwood P. Hallowell would become commander of the Fifty-Fifth Massachusetts Regiment of Infantry, also a Negro regiment, and Edward N. Hallowell would become Shaw's second in command.

Stafford Courthouse in Virginia, about forty miles south of Washington, not far from the banks of the Potomac. He wrote Andrew to that effect. As he traveled the tracks of the New Jersey Railroad, passed the winking lights of Philadelphia and in the early morning hours of February 3 rode through the now peaceful city of Baltimore, it is not likely that he was tortured by indecision in conveying Andrew's offer to hs son. Rob's contribution to the success of such a venture would be an extension of Francis Shaw's own life's work. His only reservation about his son had been expressed in his letter to Governor Andrew. "The only fear I have is in regard to his opinion of his own competency. In all other points I know he is right and true."

In Washington, Francis Shaw boarded a small steamer that carried him down the chilly Potomac to Aquia Landing where he took a train to Brooke's Station, a whistle stop about three miles from camp. He walked rutted roads from the railroad station until he saw the tents through the pines. The camp had taken on that air of semipermanence marking many a camp in Virginia that winter. A few log huts had been built and others were going up. The tents, on their plank floors, sprawled over the stump-ridden field. Everything was wallowing in mud. Francis Shaw sought out his son and gave him Governor Andrew's letter. At first Shaw was not inclined to accept. He thought the offer a great honor but felt not equal to the task. He loved his regiment and was sure of promotion where he stood. William James pointed out many years later, "In this new negro-soldier venture, loneliness was certain, ridicule inevitable, failure possible; and Shaw was only twenty-five; and although he had stood among the bullets at Cedar Mountain and Antietam, he had till then been walking socially on the sunny side of life."

Shaw talked to his father about his family and asked about Annie. Francis Shaw, as befitted him, reasoned gently with his son. Shaw's father stayed in camp that night. Before the two men retired, Francis Shaw thought his son might have a change of heart. Captain Shaw almost certainly talked to Morse about the offer and probably had a sleepless night. The next morning Shaw told his father he would not accept the Governor's offer. He sat down at his camp desk and penned a letter of refusal. Francis Shaw pocketed the letter and returned to Washington where he signed the register at Willard's Hotel and dispatched a telegram to his wife.

As soon as she had read her husband's words, Mrs. Shaw wrote

Governor Andrew, "I just received a telegram from Mr. Shaw saying, 'Rob declines. I think rightly.'" Mrs. Shaw continued, "This decision has caused me the bitterest disappointment I have ever experienced. . . ." She said that if her son had accepted the trust, "It would have been the proudest moment of my life and I could have died satisfied that I had not lived in vain. This being the truth, you will believe that I have shed bitter tears over his refusal." Then, taking a cut at her husband, she wrote, "I do not understand it unless from a habit inherited from his Father, of self-distrust in his own capabilities."

As his father left him, Shaw was dogged by uncertainty. He had made his decision out of personal considerations. His bride-to-be was very much on his mind. He treasured the little vignette which she had sent him. He took comfort in her picture in his hour of indecision but he wasn't sure he would have her support if he changed his mind. He wrote her, "Please tell me, without reserve what you think about it; for I am anxious to know."

Shaw's men loved and respected him. He had won many friends among the officers of his regiment, and his ready wit had enlivened many a campfire gathering. Henry Higginson remembered his "charming, easy frank manners, and gay yet thoughtful ways."

While Shaw's loyalty to his men, the friendships he had formed, his memory of departed comrades-in-arms bound him to his regiment, there were elements in his character pulling him strongly toward acceptance of the assignment. Besides his feeling that, as a practical measure, Negro regiments should be brought into service from Northern states as soon as possible, and his awareness that now at last the Administration smiled—however frostily—on the arming of blacks, Shaw had a natural sympathy for the Negro people which had been deepened by his encounters with slaves in Maryland and Virginia.

Since the war began, there had been widespread prejudice in the ranks of Federal regiments against the enlistment of Negroes. The belief prevailed that Negro troops would be cowardly troops. True, some Billy Yanks gave voice to practical sentiments in a marching ditty that went like this:

> In battle's wild commotion
> I won't at all object
> If a nigger should stop a bullet
> Coming for me direct.

But even practical-minded men, anxious to put Negroes to work, failed to realize that they could become magnificent fighters. If the men of a colored regiment should fail, as for various reasons many white regiments had done, their failure would be attributed to their race.

The Confederate Congress had not yet passed the act decreeing that white officers leading Negroes in battle would be considered as inciting servile insurrection and damning such men to punishment or death. But it was widely understood that such treatment might be expected. And Negro fighters would have to be told that if wounded they might be summarily shot, if captured they might be enslaved.[2]

Shaw was drawn to difficult assignments and he was probably tempted rather than deterred by the risks involved. He had proven himself capable of great physical and mental courage. A talk with his commanding officer resolved his doubts about his competence and, that afternoon, he had a change of heart. He telegraphed his father:

PLEASE DESTROY MY LETTER AND TELEGRAPH TO THE GOVERNOR THAT I ACCEPT.   STAFFORD COURT HOUSE, FEB. 5, 1863.

On hearing the news, his mother wrote him, "God rewards a hundred-fold every good aspiration of his children, and this is my reward for asking [for] my children not earthly honors, but souls to see the right and courage to follow it. Now I feel ready to die, for I see you willing to give your support to the cause of truth that is lying crushed and bleeding." Mrs. Shaw had words of praise for

---

[2] In the proclamation of outlawry issued by Jefferson Davis December 23, 1862, against the command of Major General Benjamin Butler, it had been stated that "all negro slaves if captured in arms be at once delivered over to the executive authorities of the respective States to which they belong, to be dealt with according to the laws of said States." On May 1, 1863, the Confederate Congress would pass a resolution referring directly to officers commanding Negro troops. This resolution would state that such officers would be "deemed as inciting servile insurrection, and shall, if captured be put to death or be otherwise punished. . . ." Thereafter the resolution would repeat the substance of the above provision of Davis's earlier proclamation. Though this resolution had not yet been passed, Shaw and other white officers considering service in Negro regiments knew enough to expect no quarter from Confederate officers in the field. Such remained the case until after Shaw's death when Lincoln, on July 30, 1863, finally promised retaliation "upon the enemy's prisoners in our hands" for outrages against any and all Federal soldiers and their officers.

Shaw's fiancé. "Annie too, is lovely and has shown a true, noble and right spirit."

In a spirit of resolution Shaw wrote Annie: "You know by this time, perhaps, that I have changed my mind about the black regiment. After Father left, I began to think I had made a mistake in refusing Governor Andrew's offer. Mother has telegraphed me that you would not disapprove of it, and that makes me feel much more easy about having taken it. Going for another three years is not nearly so bad a thing for a colonel as for a captain; as the former can much more easily get a furlough. Then, after I have undertaken this work, I shall feel that what I have to do is to prove that a negro can be made a good soldier, and, that being established, it will not be a point of honour with me to see the war through, unless I really occupied a position of importance in the army . . . surely those at home, who are not brave or patriotic enough to enlist should not ridicule, or throw obstacles in the way of men who are going to fight for them. . . .

"At any rate I shall not be frightened out of it by its unpopularity; and I hope you won't care if it is made fun of . . . I feel convinced I shall never regret having taken this step, as far as I myself am concerned; for while I was undecided I felt ashamed of myself, as if I were cowardly.

"Goodbye dear Annie. I hope that when I arrive at Sue's door you will not be very far off.

"With a great deal of love, (more every day) . . ."

In another letter, he wrote his father, "I have not wavered at all, since my final decision." Then, with apparent foresight, "I feel that if we can get the men, all will go right."

Charles Russell Lowell wrote to his mother, "You will be very glad to hear that Bob Shaw is to be Colonel and Norwood Hallowell Lieutenant-Colonel of the Governor's Negro Regiment. It is very important that it should be started soberly and not spoilt by too much fanaticism. Bob Shaw is not a fanatic."

Before he left Virginia, Shaw and Charles Morse visited Henry Lee Higginson, their old comrade-in-arms who had left the Second to serve in the First Massachusetts Cavalry. The First lay in camp before Fredericksburg, about fifteen miles southwest of Stafford Courthouse on the banks of the Rappahannock River. Higginson remembered seeing the two men ride up to the little log house where he lived with Greely Curtis. "We four had marched from Boston together, and were held together by strong bonds. Robert Shaw, who was very fond of Greely Curtis, came to tell us that he was going home to be Colonel of the 54th Massachusetts Infantry, colored. This was great news, indeed a real event in our lives, for we all knew how much Robert cared for his old comrades, and how contrary to his wishes this was.

"We troopers expressed our strong approval and sympathy with his action, which greatly pleased him, for at that date plenty of good people frowned on the use of colored troops. Bob said, 'Governor Andrew asked me and I am going; but if either of you fellows will go, I'll gladly serve under you. I don't want the higher rank.' We should have been glad to serve under him, but had our duty to perform in our own regiment; and so we could only bid him good-by."

After stopping in New York for a reunion with Annie and his family, Shaw arrived in Boston on February 15. The following day he met Andrew and liked him immediately. In the morning Shaw and Andrew went for a ride through the frosty streets of Boston in the Governor's carriage. Andrew was short and rotund, a man of immense energy. Shaw found him a person of practical good sense, charming and kindhearted. Andrew had been stirred by antislavery sentiments while still a boy. He had been admitted to the bar in 1840, had always been public-spirited. He had practiced criminal law. A brilliant speech in the Massachuetts Legislature in the session of 1858, had at once made him a leader of the Republican party. As chairman to the Massachusetts delegation to the Republican National Convention at Chicago, he had worked for the nomination of Lincoln. In spite of Lincoln's moderate approach to slavery and the enlistment of Negroes in the armed forces, Andrew held him in the highest regard.

For his projected regiment, Andrew had thought first of recruiting Negroes at Port Royal and in other Southern coastal regions as General Hunter had done. He had proposed to Stanton that General Butler, no longer in Louisiana, be put in charge of the job, but Butler had been out of favor with Stanton and when the irrepressible Andrew had been turned down, he had bounced back with the suggestion that he be authorized to raise a Negro regiment in his own state.

From *The Monument to Robert Gould Shaw*
Houghton Mifflin Co., 1897.

Augustus St. Gaudens's monument to Robert Gould Shaw
and his regiment. Unveiled in Boston in 1897.

Sketch by the author

ROBERT GOULD SHAW

The house at 44 Beacon Street as it is today.

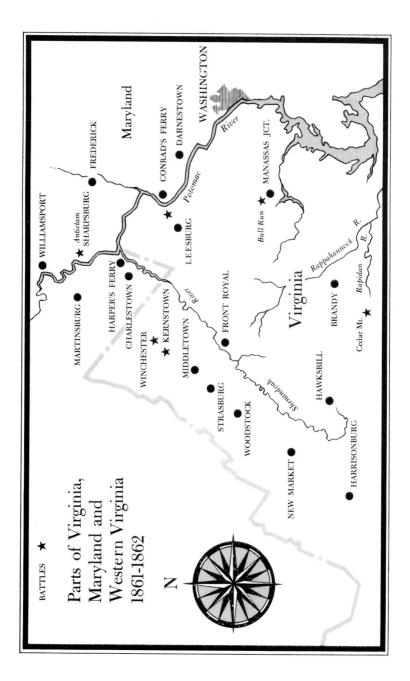

Parts of Virginia,
Maryland and
Western Virginia
1861-1862

BATTLES ★

N

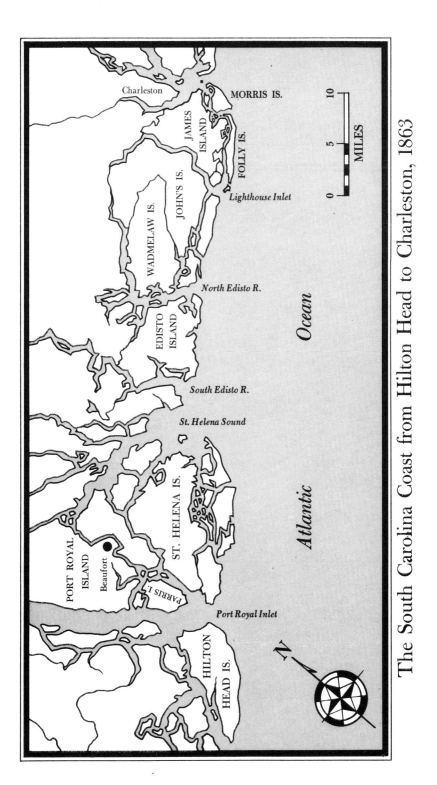

The South Carolina Coast from Hilton Head to Charleston, 1863

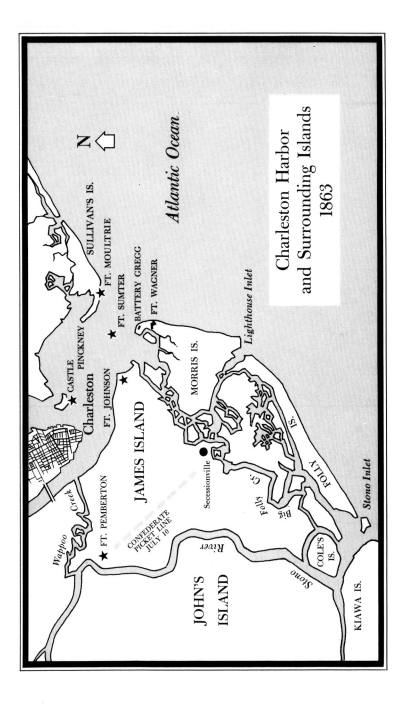

Charleston Harbor
and Surrounding Islands
1863

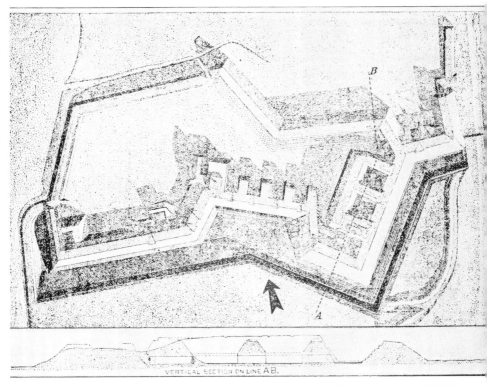

VERTICAL SECTION ON LINE A B.

Adapted from a diagram on p. 29, *Official Records . . . Series I, Vol. XXVIII, Part I.*

Fort Wagner, sometimes called Battery Wagner, was one of the strongest earthworks ever built. The arrow indicates the point at which Shaw and the leading elements of his regiment hit the curtain.

Dead soldiers at Fort Wagner.
Sketch by Frank Vizetelly, 1830-1883.

Andrew had started recruiting on the optimistic assumption that a full regiment of Negroes might be raised in Massachusetts, but this would soon prove an impossibility. Joseph Kennedy, superintendent of the census, would soon come forward with the estimate that, if Negroes of military age enlisted at the same rate as their white brothers, Massachusetts could supply no more than 394 Negroes for the Fifty-Fourth.

On the day of the meeting of Shaw and Andrew, a notice appeared in the *Boston Journal*:

TO COLORED MEN

Wanted. Good men for the Fifty-Fourth Regiment of Massachusetts Volunteers of African descent, Col. Robert G. Shaw (commanding). $100 bounty at expiration of term of service. Pay $13 per month,[3] and State aid for families. All necessary information can be obtained at the office, corner Cambridge and North Russell Streets.

LIEUT. J. W. M. APPLETON,
Recruiting Officer.

Appleton, a person of energy and sanguine temperament, had been the first man commissioned in the Fifty-Fourth.

Just before Shaw's arrival in Boston, Andrew had appointed a committee of wealthy and influential men to supervise the raising of colored troops. The committee included such men as George L. Stearns, a ships' chandler who, like Andrew, had helped finance the activities of John Brown, Amos A. Lawrence, long a worker in the antislavery crusade, Shaw's father Francis George Shaw, John M. Forbes, whom Robert Shaw had visited at Naushon in 1859, and a handful of others of similar persuasion. The membership was later increased to 100 and became known as the "Black Committee."[4]

Andrew told Shaw his plans and, in the afternoon, Shaw went to work at the State House "looking over papers with Hallowell,

---

[3] This was the same pay received by white soldiers. The Federal government customarily paid their soldiers bounties in advance but did not do so in the case of the Fifty-Fourth. On May 18, 1863, rolls were made up for payment of a state bounty to the men of Shaw's regiment. This they received. In Chapter Fifteen on page 115 and in a footnote on pages 115, 116, Shaw's, Andrew's and Edward Hallowell's troubles over pay are outlined further.

[4] Beside those mentioned in the text, the original roster of the Black Committee included these names: William I. Bowditch, Le Baron Russell, Richard P. Hallowell (brother of the young officers), Mayor Howland and James B. Congdon of New Bedford and Willard P. Phillips of Salem.

and talking with Andrew. We have decided to go into camp at Readville. . . ."

Shaw liked Hallowell and the two men got along "in the pleasantest way." Like Shaw, Hallowell was battle-tested. Andrew had described him as "a gallant and fine fellow, true as steel to the cause of humanity, as well as the flag of the Country." Hallowell's father, Morris L. Hallowell, had made his house in Philadelphia "a hospital and home for Massachusetts officers. . . ." He was an ardent antislavery man and had passed his sentiments along to his sons, two of whom were now officers in the Fifty-Fourth and one a merchant in Boston. The latter was a member of the Black Committee.

During these early days Shaw busied himself interviewing prospective officers, taking only the best from the flood that applied. As the choosing of officers began, Andrew was heard to remark to a friend that in regard to other regiments, he had accepted as officers men who were sometimes rough and uncultivated, but these soldiers, Andrew said, "shall be commanded by officers who are eminently gentlemen."

One of the finest of those who applied was William H. Simkins of West Roxbury. Simkins wrote at the time of his acceptance, "This is no hasty conclusion, no blind leap of an enthusiast, but the result of much hard thinking. It will not be at first, and probably not for a long time, an agreeable position, for many reasons too evident to state. . . . Then this is nothing but an experiment after all; but it is an experiment that I think it is high time we should try,—an experiment which, the sooner we prove fortunate the sooner we can count upon an immense number of hardy troops that can stand the effect of a Southern climate without injury; an experiment which the sooner we prove unsuccessful, the sooner we shall establish an important truth and rid ourselves of a false hope." Simkins, like Shaw, would give his life to prove the experiment "fortunate."

Lieutenant Appleton set to work recruiting Negroes. On the evening of the day after Shaw met Andrew, a rally was held in Joy Street Church. Edward L. Pierce, a graduate of Harvard Law School who had been superintendent of the Port Royal Project, was one of the speakers. He called on the Negroes present to "stand by those who for half a century had maintained that they [the Negroes] would prove brave and patriotic men when the opportunity came."

Wendell Phillips mounted the rostrum amid something close to an ovation. Phillips was an accomplished public speaker. "Now they offer you a musket and say, 'Come and help us.' The question is, will you of Massachusetts take hold? I hear there is some reluctance because you are not to have officers of your own color. This may be wrong, for I think you have as much right to the first commission in a brigade as a white man. No regiment should be without a mixture of the races. But if you cannot have a whole loaf, will you not take a slice?"

Phillips went on to explain that white officers would meet with less prejudice in organizing and commanding such a regiment, that a cadre of white officers would be better able to contend with the inevitable difficulties to be encountered. He reminded them that they could earn commissions in the field. "Put yourselves under the stars and stripes, and fight yourselves to the marquee of a general, and you shall come out with a sword." This remark was greeted by cheers.

Shaw himself, in spite of frequent appearances before his men in the Second Massachusetts and his debating experience of Harvard days, had something of a horror of speaking at public gatherings and he did not appear. Norwood Hallowell spoke in his place. Other speakers followed Hallowell and that eminent gentleman from Rochester, New York, Negro leader Frederick Douglass, whose war cry was, "Action! Action!" stirred the audience to further applause. "We can get at the throat of treason and slavery through the State of Massachusetts. She was first in the War of Independence; first to break the chains of her slaves; first to make the black man equal before the law; first to admit colored children to her common schools. She was first to answer with her blood the alarm-cry of the nation when its capitol was menaced by the Rebels. You know her patriotic Governor, and you know Charles Sumner. I need add no more. Massachusetts now welcomes you as her soldiers."

Recruiting began with high hopes. Edward N. Hallowell, Norwood's brother, who would be commissioned major of the Fifty-Fourth, had done some recruiting outside Massachusetts. In Philadelphia, in company with two other men, he had brought in a handful of recruits. His efforts had been attended by difficulties. Philadelphia in the 1860's was the home of some virulent racist sentiment. The gathering place was kept secret and the men were sent to Massachusetts in small groups, under cover of night. Funds were low and Robert R. Corson, the Massachusetts State Agent who was helping Hallowell, was obliged to purchase tickets for some of the men with his own pocket money.

New Bedford had been chosen as a fertile field for recruiting. A young businessman named James W. Grace, who had been commissioned February 10, had opened a recruiting office on Williams Street near the post office. Grace saw no need to be secretive. He hoisted a United States flag outside the office, enlisted the help of Negro preachers and asked Wendell Phillips, Frederick Douglass and others to come to town to speak on behalf of the regiment.

Lieutenant Grace was openly insulted and told that Negroes would turn at the first sight of an enemy. He was shouted at in the streets, "There goes the captain of the Negro Company!" Grace's little son was made fun of in school because his father was raising a company of black men to fight whites.

The men who rallied to Grace's call were a healthy lot ranging in age from sixteen to their late thirties. About a dozen had been laborers, half a dozen seamen and there was a scattering of others including a waiter and a barber. The New Bedford men and a number of farmers and laborers from other parts of Massachusetts formed the nucleus of Company C. Their backgrounds were similar to those of men who were forming and would form the other companies of the Fifty-Fourth.

Before he went to stay at Readville, Shaw lived with his Sturgis relatives at 44 Beacon Street. The windows of his room faced the bare trees and winter grass of Boston Common where he had sometimes romped when he was a child. As he started work, he wrote to Annie, "Do write often, Annie dear, for I need a word occasionally from those whom I love, to keep up my courage."

In the mornings, Shaw walked briskly up Beacon Street to the State House, whose dome rose above the leafless elms and lindens, to the rooms where he would work with Hallowell and the Governor, whom he liked "more and more every day. . . ."

Shaw wrote to his father to find Negro leaders in New York and Brooklyn who would help with recruiting. He suggested that there should be ". . . no noise about it, as New York authorities might object to our taking them from there. No recruiting office should be opened."

On February 21, while Shaw worked in Boston, Ned Hallowell took a handful of men to Camp Meigs at Readville. Readville was on the Boston and Providence Railroad, a few miles south of the city in the center of a broad plain. In spring and summer the plain had a pleasant aspect, its rich meadows were studded with great elms and in the distance were the pine-covered slopes of the Blue Hill of Milton. But in winter the camp was a bleak and cheerless place. The flat ground made good drill fields, but when the weather was wet the slender streams that traced their courses through the meadows overflowed their banks and turned the plain to a sea of mud. The barracks, in military rows, were great wooden structures with sleeping bunks on either side. The officers were quartered in smaller buildings of the same character. The larger part of the Second Massachusetts Cavalry under Charles Russell Lowell was encamped at Readville. Since Lowell himself was sympathetic to the Governor's project and admired Shaw, no trouble was expected from his white troopers.

While Hallowell set up camp, Shaw champed at the bit. He was eager to take charge of the regiment himself. "All my mornings are spent in the State House; and as in-door, furnace-heated work does not agree with me, I shall get out to Readville as soon as possible."

Shaw's evenings were pleasant. He wrote to Charles Morse, "I have been to a dinner or small party almost every day since I got to Boston and have enjoyed myself." Then, referring to Annie, "Amazingly though, my mind wanders to a certain person in N. Y."

One evening Shaw visited his Aunt Susan Parkman, of whom he had written ten years before from Neuchâtel, "She seems to have a pretty good opinion of me, and if I hear much more of such praise I shall begin to *think* I'm somebody." Mrs. Parkman's only son had been killed less than two months before, fighting in Virginia. Shaw was saddened by the visit. His aunt and other members of the family "talked of Theodore a great deal, and seemed to find great comfort in it. . . ." Then Shaw had some cheerful news for his mother. "They thought I had done a good thing in taking the Fifty-Fourth Massachusetts. About this I have only good words from friends and foes of the project. . . ."

Early in March Shaw wrote of his last "furnace heated" ordeal: "At 2 P.M. I was informed I must meet and confer with a committee of ladies who wished to do something to assist the Fifty-Fourth Massachusetts. At 4 o'clock, I proceeded with a light heart and jaunty step to Bowdoin Street, where the four ladies composing the committee were supposed to be in session.

"I rang the bell, the door opened; I hung up my coat in the entry, and stepping to the parlour, a fearful sight met my terrified gaze. There sat what seemed to me about seventeen thousand ladies and two men. The ladies were of all ages, but the majority were on the down side. If I could possibly have bolted, I should have made the attempt; but it was useless. I was brought forward to the slaughter in a terrible perspiration, and if I had not been able to recover myself while being introduced to the audience, I don't know if I should have pulled through. As it was I managed to give a brief account of what progress had been made in my regiment, and what articles the men were in need of. Friday, I am invited to attend a meeting in commemoration of the death of Crispus Attucks;[5] but I shall make Hallowell go instead, as he is a very good speaker, and has already begun in that line since we have been here. . . .

"I go out to camp tomorrow."

---

[5] Crispus Attucks, described by John Adams as almost a giant in stature, is thought to have been the leader of the mob which precipitated the Boston Massacre. Attucks was reported to have been an American Negro, but his origins are obscure. Since most of the men in the mob were seamen, he was probably a seaman. It is possible that Attucks was not an American at all but a native of the West Indies. It seems likely, however, that Attucks was an escaped American slave because, some years before his death, a Massachusetts slave-owner had reported the loss of a slave with a similar name. At any rate, rascal or saint, free Negro or slave, he was shot and killed by a British soldier.

11.

Shaw had mixed feelings about his first day at Readville. The barracks had been scrubbed down and the men were neat and proud in their uniforms, already presenting a soldierly appearance. The uniforms had "pleased them amazingly." But the place was bleak. Shaw wrote to Charlie Morse that everything was "topsy turvy—nothing to eat and the coldest possible barracks."

Shaw wrote to Morse about some new recruits. "34 came up from New Bedford this afternoon and marched with drum and fife creating the greatest enthusiasm among the rest—we had them examined, sworn in, washed and uniformed as soon as they arrived—and when they get into their buttons they feel about as good as men can—it is very laughable to hear the sergeants explain the drill to the men, as they use words long enough for a doctor of divinity. . . ."

The regimental historian described the recruits: "Only a small proportion had been slaves. There were a large number of comparatively light-complexioned men. In stature they reached the average of white volunteers. Compared with the material of contraband regiments, they were lighter, taller, of more regular features." There were qualified clerks and men who could be trained to do the duties of warrant officers. Massachusetts Surgeon General Dale examined the recruits himself. He reported, "The first recruits were sent to Camp Meigs, Readville, in February, 1863; their medical examination was most rigid and thorough, nearly one third of the number offered being peremptorily rejected. As a consequence, a more robust, strong, and healthy a set of men were never mustered into the service of the United States."

Shaw agreed that physical standards should be high, though such a policy would fill the ranks slowly. Shaw knew that if standards were slack he would find himself commanding a dwindling regiment in the field.

The Surgeon General's report continued, "The barracks, cookhouses, and kitchens far surpassed in cleanliness any I have ever witnessed, and were models of neatness and good order. The cooks, . . . had many of them been in similar employment in other places, and had therefore brought some skill to the present responsibility.

"In camp, these soldiers presented a buoyant cheerfulness and hilarity. . . ."

The optimism of these early days was dampened by the slowness with which recruits appeared in camp. During the last week in February, Andrew and George L. Stearns of the Black Committee had a talk at the State House. Stearns, a Medford man, had contributed to the work in Kansas, had supported the raid on Harper's Ferry and had been an early champion of Negro enlistment. A year or so before, he had been silenced by groans and hisses in the Town Hall of Medford when he had advocated the arming of blacks. Stearns, like Andrew a man of boundless energy, had already succeeded in raising some money for the regiment, had supervised the opening of recruiting offices in Massachusetts and had set up clandestine recruiting activities outside the state. But Negroes were not flocking to the fold and Andrew was an impatient man. When he had expressed his disappointment to Stearns, Stearns had said, "I will get you a regiment."

Andrew had asked, "How do you propose to do it?"

"I shall go to Canada and see what can be done among the fugitives there. After that I will explore the western states."

"When will you start?"

"Tomorrow morning."

Stearns was as good as his word. He left his business in the hands of subordinates so he could devote full time to the effort. One of his first stops was in Rochester, New York, where he enlisted Frederick Douglass's son, Lewis, who later became sergeant major of the regiment.[1] Stearns wasn't modest. "I have worked every day, Sundays included . . . and from fourteen to eighteen hours of every one of those days. I have filled the West with my agents; have forced the railroad to accept my terms of transportation; have filled a letter-book of five hundred pages with my correspondence, most of it closely written, and have borrowed $10,000 on my own responsibility to meet my payments."

---

[1] Charles R. Douglass, Lewis's younger brother, joined the regiment later. He was mustered in April 18, 1863, at age nineteen.

Stearns recruited in Canada, New York State, western Pennsylvania, Ohio, Indiana, Missouri, Illinois and Michigan. In states where the public was hostile to the enlistment of Negroes, he shepherded small groups of men to the railroad depots under cover of night, as Hallowell had done in Philadelphia. While engaged in recruiting in Buffalo, Stearns wrote "I am doing a work that no one else can. No one living could at this moment move the black man as I am moving him, except the man who dares not. What a response would they give to a call from Abraham Lincoln. Nothing could stop them; they would rush from every hole and corner, desert any occupation, make any sacrifice. . . . These men are as capable as whites of taking care of themselves and on the whole are more honest and disinterested."

Ostensibly, no recruiting was done outside Massachusetts but it was an open secret that Andrew's agents were working far and wide. *The National Intelligencer* poked fun at Andrew, reporting that he had "opened recruiting offices at New York, Philadelphia, Fortress Monroe, and even as far southwards as Key West." The *Intelligencer* quoted a nameless humorist from New York. "His crimping sergeants will shortly turn up in Egypt, competing with Napoleon for the next cargo of Nubians."

Such derision, especially from the conservative *Intelligencer*, if noted at all by Andrew and Stearns, must have pleased this pair of activists. They had waited long for their chance to raise a Negro regiment and now that they had it they were bound to go forward with their plans.

While Stearns and his lieutenants roamed the countryside, sleeping on trains, waiting at stations, eating meals when they could, sometimes taking supper with Negro families, sometimes dining in hotels, Shaw's voice rang across the meadows at Readville as he taught his men the rudiments of soldiering. The growing regiment and its young commander were making news. Passengers on the Boston and Providence line looked out at the great sprawling camp with gathering interest. There was criticism to right and left. The skeptics shook their heads and said that Negroes would never make fighters. And even those who instinctively felt that generations of slavery, of being pressed into the role of helot, had not permanently crippled American Negro manhood asked how Negroes could fight when they knew that if captured they would be returned to slavery and if wounded they might be summarily shot. And, from the other side, from gentle-hearted humanitarians, unfamiliar with the discipline of army life, came complaints that Shaw was treating his black men harshly. Shaw, knowing that such rumors would sadden his mother, wrote to her, "You may be perfectly certain that any reports of cruelty are entirely untrue." He assured his mother that he treated the men of the Fifty-Fourth far less harshly than he had treated his men in the Second Massachusetts Infantry.

Shaw, biting into his job at last, worked tirelessly. Soon after his arrival at camp, the regiment, now consisting of four companies, was driven indoors by snow and cold and winds that swept the meadows. But in cramped barracks the drilling went on.

On March 17, Shaw wrote, "Men come in every day. Mr. Stearns, who is at home for a few days from Canada, says we can get more men than we want from there."

For more than a month, the Governor's optimism would be quite contained, but Shaw, catching some of Stearns's boundless supply, began to be even more selective than before. He wrote his father, "Don't you think Brown[2] had better give up his office in New York? We get finer men from the country and there is no doubt of our filling up pretty rapidly." Shaw then inserted a weather note. "The snow is deep, and making a good layer of mud for us."

On March 25, Shaw wrote Amos A. Lawrence, one of the members of the Black Committee, "We are getting along finely and expect to have 400 men in camp this week—"

Several days later, still full of sunshine, he wrote to his mother, praising the intelligence of his men and revealing no small measure of assurance and pride. "There is not the least doubt that we will leave the State with as good a regiment as any that has marched."

Officers from other regiments came to Readville to look things over. One of them was a mustering officer, a Virginian who had thrown in his lot with the Federal cause. He had thought it a great joke to make soldiers of the "niggers" but a look at Shaw's regiment changed his mind. Shaw wrote, "The skeptics need only to come out here to be converted."

Shaw and Annie had decided to marry before the regiment formed line at Readville for the last time. Early in March he had

---

[2] W. Wells Brown: Negro leader in New York City who was recruiting men for the Fifty-Fourth.

visited her in New York. Now, late in the month, Annie came to Boston to be near him. Shaw's mother was opposed to an early marriage and the Haggertys had objected too. Shaw wrote, "Annie has not been well since she came here. In one way it has been very fortunate, for we have had several quiet evenings together."

Shaw's mother felt that marriage would take her son's mind off his work, that he might be tempted to take advantage of his rank to take Annie with him when the regiment left camp. When she wrote him to this effect, his answer was firm. He wrote, "I received your letter last evening, and you must excuse me for saying, I didn't think your arguments very powerful. If I thought that being married were going to make me neglect my duty, I should think it much better never to have been engaged. As for Annie's going out with me, I don't think such a thing would ever enter my head. It is the last thing I should desire, as I have seen the evil consequences of it very often." His mother had suggested that they wait six months. Shaw continued, "The chances of my coming home in six months are very small. . . . Indeed, one reason for my wishing to be married is that we are going to undertake a very dangerous piece of work and I feel that there are more chances than ever of my not getting back. I know I should go away happy and contented if we were married. I showed Annie your letter. . . ."

Several days later, with a snowstorm raging outside his window, he wrote that "if we are not married before I go, I shall feel very much dissatisfied and discontented. For the sake of Annie's and my own peace of mind, I want it."

As the ranks of the Fifty-Fourth were filled and Shaw's work was noticed by a number of Boston's leading citizens, curiosity burned in the breast of handsome patriarch Josiah Quincy. Quincy, born before the American Revolution, had been known as "Old Quin" when President of Harvard. After resigning the presidency of the college, he had complained that "the unearthly quiet of city streets, in contrast to the turbulent college yard, kept him awake o' nights." Quincy, too old and sick to go to Readville, invited Shaw to visit him.

Shaw wrote to his brother-in-law, George Curtis, of the visit. "The other day I called on Mr. Josiah Quincy, *Seniorissimo.* and had a very interesting visit. . . . He talked a good deal of events which happened in the last century, and which I was delighted to hear about. He had an engraving of Uncle Sam,[3] hanging at the head of his bed, and referred to him continually during my visit. He seemed to recollect him with a sort of veneration. He said, 'I shook hands with him last, on the wharf, when he sailed for China in seventeen hundred and—something.'

"What a beautiful head and face Mr. Quincy has! I sat and looked at him in perfect wonder, as I thought of the men he had known, and the events he had had an active part in."

By May 1, there were signs of spring on Readville's meadows. The elms were touched with delicate green and under a cobalt sky distant steeples and factory chimneys gleamed in the strengthening sun. The parade ground had dried, and columns of blue-coated Negroes drilled with precision and went about their familiar duties. Men were still coming in, but now the ranks of the regiment were nearly full.

Stearns's long winter of tireless work had borne its fruit and Shaw and his officers had seen a regiment come into being. Governor Andrew was pleased with Stearns's success but, in view of the trouble that had been encountered raising men for the Fifty-Fourth, he had decided that no attempt should be made to raise another Negro regiment. He telegraphed the traveling Stearns to that effect and Stearns answered exuberantly:

> I HAVE 200 MEN TOWARD A FIFTY FIFTH.
> WHAT SHALL I DO WITH THEM?

Andrew gave Stearns four weeks to raise the balance and it was done.

---

[3] Major Samuel Shaw. The engraving Shaw refers to was probably the one which appears on the frontispiece of Major Shaw's journals published in 1847. This engraving depicts an aristocratic, roughish-looking man with a fine head of silken hair framing a rather young face. When he sat for his portrait, he wore clothes that were meticulously tailored, a dark velvet coat with buttons to match and a gleaming white silk vest and stock.

12.

On a soft spring night, in gentle seas, Shaw traveled by steamer from Boston to New York, arriving on the morning of May 1 to prepare for his wedding the following day at the Church of the Ascension at Fifth Avenue and Tenth Street. To please his mother he carried in his luggage a full-dress colonel's uniform, but he had written her that he would feel like a jackass if he wore it at the wedding.

The simple, elegant brownstone church was set in a neighborhood of fine eighteenth-century houses, red brick with slate roofs, their window frames, sashes and doors painted white, their brass knockers and lanterns gleaming. In the high, dark interior of the church, sunlight filtered through amber leaded glass, set in slim Gothic windows. Shaw and Haggerty sisters, cousins and aunts were there and a liberal scattering of friends. The bride wore her traveling dress and carried a small bouquet. Shaw, ignoring his mother's pleas to deck himself out like a soldier in a comic opera, wore civilian clothes. The Reverend Cotton Smith, standing in front of a bank of flowers, intoned the familiar words. Annie's father, Ogden Haggerty, gave his daughter away.

After the wedding, as Shaw and Annie stepped into the bright sunlight, war must have seemed a million miles away. The budding trees along the edge of Washington Parade Ground were hosts to nesting sparrows, mockingbirds and cardinals. As Shaw and his bride climbed into a waiting carriage, the twitter of sparrows rose above the squeak of wheels and the clatter of hooves on the busy avenue.

The bride and groom and members of the wedding party made their way north to Twenty-Third Street to the dazzling, thickly-carpeted Fifth Avenue Hotel where tables, under chandeliers that looked like clusters of white grapes, were covered with the finest linen, set with gleaming silver and the best crystal in the house. After the wedding feast, the couple entrained for Lenox where they would spend the first days of their honeymoon at Ogden Haggerty's Massachusetts farm.

Early in the evening, on the first day of his honeymoon, Shaw penned a brief note to Charlie Morse, telling him of his marriage. Shaw said he could imagine Morse and his other friends in camp by a "rail fire." He wrote, "Just now I am very differently occupied, for I was married yesterday and have come up here for a week. . . .

"The country is just beginning to look green and the weather perfect— We are living at Pa Haggerty's place which is a remarkably pretty one and I expect to have as nice a time as one in the same circumstances ever did—saddle horses and a light waggon are on hand, when we want to ride or drive and a nice garden and pine grove near to furnish pleasant walks."

Shaw wrote touchingly of Morse's sister who was a guest at the wedding. "I don't think I ever saw a sweeter face than your sister's and if her lameness has had anything to do with forming such a beautiful character as she must have, it is not too dear a price to pay for it."

While in Lenox, Shaw wrote to his sister, Josephine, "I have been in quite an angelic mood ever since we got here. . . ." He wrote that his bliss had been shattered by a telegram from Norwood Hallowell, in command of the regiment in Shaw's absence. The telegram brought the news that Andrew planned to send the regiment off on the twentieth. Shaw wrote, "O how glum I feel!"

His gloom deepened when he learned that Norwood Hallowell would remain at Readville to command the projected Fifty-Fifth. Both Hallowells had refused the colonelcy of the Fifty-Fifth, preferring to stay with Shaw, but Andrew had pressed Norwood Hallowell into the job. Ned Hallowell, a handsome broad-shouldered man with drooping mustaches, who had served for a time on Frémont's staff, would stay with Shaw, becoming Lieutenant Colonel of the Fifty-Fourth.

From Lenox, Shaw and Annie crossed the state by train to Boston, then went to Readville where Shaw had found quarters at a pleasant boarding house half a mile from camp where the couple had "a private table and parlour and everything else."

By May 14, the ranks of the Fifty-Fourth were full. The men of the regiment, one thousand strong, had been supplied with En-field rifles. Some of the noncommissioned officers had been equipped with swords. To most of them, drilling was second nature by now. Not only had they taken to the rudiments of army life, but they had gained for themselves a reputation for excellent behavior. Surgeon General Dale had reported that the men were "gentlemen as well as soldiers."

May 18 dawned fine and clear—the day set aside for the presentation of colors. During the morning, friends of the regiment arrived at Readville in carriages and by train. Among the guests were William Lloyd Garrison, Wendell Phillips and Negro leader Frederick Douglass whose sons were members of the regiment. The locomotive of the morning train to Readville had pulled nine extra cars, added to accommodate the friends and families of officers and men.

At eleven o'clock, Shaw's voice rang out, commanding the regiment to form. Four flags were ready for presentation. They were brilliant in color and of the finest texture, fluttering in the fresh breeze. One of the flags, a cross on a blue field containing the motto "In Hoc Signo Vinces," had been presented by friends of Lieutenant Willie Lowell Putnam, fatally wounded near Wendell Holmes at Ball's Bluff. As the men settled into their positions, the last rifle sling creaked and Governor Andrew took his position in front of the formation. There was a prayer by Negro pastor Rev. Leonard A. Grimes and the Governor stepped forward and made a speech in rich Victorian prose, garnished with noble sentiment. He spoke of the regiment as having been, for many months, the desire of his heart. He said, "I stand or fall as a man and a magistrate, with the rise and fall in history of the Fifty-Fourth Massachusetts Regiment." Speaking of the men in the ranks, Andrew asserted that their opportunity was "an opportunity for a whole race of men."

Turning to Shaw, the Governor said, "I know not, Sir, when in all human history, to any given thousands of men in arms, there has been committed a work at once so proud, so precious, so full of hope and glory, as the work committed to you."

Andrew presented the colors to Shaw. As he tendered the national flag, he said, "The white stripes of its field will be red with blood before it shall be surrendered to the foe."

Shaw's response to the Governor was brief. He thanked him for the flags and said simply, "May we have an opportunity to show that you have not made a mistake in intrusting the honor of the State to a colored regiment,—the first State that has ever sent one to the war." Then he thanked his men for their faithfulness and devotion to their work.

The speeches finished, the Fifty-Fourth was reviewed by the Governor and his staff. A correspondent for the *Springfield Republican* wrote that the men were a fine lot, with an uncommon amount of muscle. "They marched well, they wheeled well, and there was about their whole array an air of completeness, order, and morale. . . ."

After the ceremony, the Governor handed Shaw a telegram from Secretary Stanton:

THE FIFTY FOURTH MASSACHUSETTS WILL REPORT TO GENERAL HUNTER. MAKE REQUISITIONS, SO THAT THEY MAY GO AT ONCE.

Major General David Hunter, an enthusiastic if bumbling promoter of Negro fighting units, had asked Stanton for the Fifty-Fourth and Stanton's decision to grant his request was a natural one. Hunter was at Hilton Head, commanding the Department of the South. Thomas Wentworth Higginson's contraband regiment, the First Regiment of South Carolina Volunteers, was now serving under Hunter. Colonel James Montgomery who, with Thomas Wentworth Higginson, had plotted to free John Brown's men at Charlestown, had been authorized by Stanton to raise a second regiment of contrabands in Hunter's department. Montgomery was now in the South with his cadre of Northern officers bagging contrabands for the Second South Carolina Volunteer Infantry. He was taking the word "volunteer" with a grain of salt.

At nine o'clock on the morning of May 28, the men of the Fifty-Fourth climbed down from the railroad cars. Shaw, who had spent the previous night with his wife in Boston, met the regiment at Providence Depot. He mounted his horse and ordered his men to form a line. The sky this late May day was deep blue, broken only by an occasional high-soaring gull or fluttering flights of smaller birds. The sun carved sharp shadows on the station platform and the cobbled streets. Shaw took his position at the head of the regiment. He was preceded by Patrick Gilmore's marching band and a large contingent of police under chief Colonel Kurtz. Unknown to the public, reserves of police were held out of sight to suppress expected rioting. The columns moved out into Boylston Street which was lined with people. There was excitement in the air and, almost at once, cheering broke out. Dr. Bowditch, a long-standing antislavery man and member of the "Black Committee," raised a cheer for Shaw as the regiment passed along Boylston Street. He wrote in his diary, "I got from him that lovely, almost heavenly smile. . . ."

Shaw and his regiment threaded their way, by a circuitous route, through the narrow, history-laden streets just west of roughly triangular Boston Common. The streets were bright with national, state and regimental colors. There was no sign of disrespect, no signal of rioting. One of the marchers remembered, "All along the route, the sidewalks, windows, and balconies were thronged with spectators, and the appearance of the regiment caused repeated cheers and waving of flags and handkerchiefs. . . ." As he passed the house of Wendell Phillips, on Essex Street, Shaw saluted William Lloyd Garrison, who was standing on Phillips's balcony, his hand resting on a bust of John Brown, tears streaming down his face. Just past Phillips's house, a woman swept into the street and thrust a bright bouquet into Shaw's hand. The columns looped around Pemberton Square. In the Somerset Club, then on Somerset Street, staid members crossed the carpets and drew the curtains against the offending sight. Other members, impatient with the bigotry of their fellows and loyal to Shaw, whom they knew as a friend, walked out in protest and joined in the cheering.[1] Shaw passed into Beacon Street where, in front of the State House, he paused to greet Governor Andrew and his staff who were then escorted down the hill.

Ellen Shaw, who watched from the second-floor balcony of the house at 44 Beacon Street, wrote later, "I was not quite eighteen when the regiment sailed. My mother, Rob's wife, my sisters and I were on the balcony to see the regiment go by, and when Rob riding at its head, looked up and kissed his sword, his face was as

---

[1] This story is probably true. It has been said that the members of the Somerset Club who walked out that day subsequently formed the Union Club. In a letter to his friend Charley Morse written at Readville on March 4, 1863, Shaw wrote that he "had an invitation to visit the Somerset Club whenever he wished, and the other evening I went in there— A great many of them are 'bloody copperheads' but no one made any disagreeable remarks while I was there. . . ." This letter is among the Shaw papers at the Massachusetts Historical Society.

the face of an angel and I felt perfectly sure he would never come back."

Frederick Douglass was in Boston that day to watch his sons march by, and John Greenleaf Whittier, pacifist though he was, came out this day for his first sight of armed men since the beginning of the war. Whittier was deeply stirred by the sight of the marching Negro soldiers but refrained from expressing his feelings in verse, "lest I should indirectly give a new impulse to war." But Whittier did write to Lydia Maria Child, "The only regiment I ever looked upon during the war was the 54th Massachusetts on its departure for the South. I can never forget the scene as Colonel Shaw rode at the head of his men. The very flower of grace and chivalry, he seemed to me beautiful and awful, as an angel of God come down to lead the host of freedom to victory."

The Common was entered by the Charles Street gate and, on the parade ground, the regiment passed in review before the Governor and the tightly packed throng. At noon, the regiment marched across the Common to the West Street gate and made its way to Battery Wharf. Shaw, still riding at the head of his regiment, moved through a corridor of madly cheering onlookers. As they entered State Street, the thunderous applause reminded Shaw of his passage with the Seventh down Broadway in April of 1861. Gilmore's band struck up John Brown's hymn to honor the memory of Crispus Attucks, of Thomas Sims, fugitive slave who was led along State Street to the Long Wharf where he was put aboard the Savannah-bound *Acorn* to be returned to slavery and of Anthony Burns, another fugitive slave who had been trooped through a silent crowd along State Street on the way back to his master in Virginia.[2]

At Battery Wharf, only family and friends were permitted to

[2] After Sims's recapture, he escaped again and found his way back to Boston where, on this day, he watched the parade of the Fifty-Fourth. Anthony Burns, born in Virginia, had been a "slave preacher." He escaped from bondage in 1854 and, in the same year, was arrested in Boston. Thomas Wentworth Higginson, in the hope of freeing Burns, led an abortive attack on Burns's prison. After having been identified by his former master, Burns was marched down State Street and put aboard a ship and sent back to Virginia. A few months after his return to Virginia, Burns was sold to a friendly master who resold him to a group of Boston citizens who freed him and sent him to school. Burns became pastor of the Zion Baptist Church at St. Catherine's in Canada.

stay with the soldiers as they stood by the side of the fine, new transport *De Molay*, waiting for the signal to board the ship. The families of most of the Negroes lived too far from Boston to be on hand and many of the soldiers just stood around and talked among themselves.

The lines were cast off and, as the transport slid away from the wharf amid the sounds of thumping engines and the brass and drums of Patrick Gilmore's band, handkerchiefs fluttered in the afternoon sun. A few friends of the regiment, including Frederick Douglass, stayed with the vessel until she was well away, then returned to the city on a shepherding tug. As the moon rose and land dropped astern, Shaw was full of pride in his regiment and confident of its success.

A few days later he wrote, "Truly I ought to be thankful for all my happiness and success in life so far; and if the raising of colored troops proves such a benefit to the country and to the blacks, . . . I shall thank God a thousand times that I was led to take my share in it."

13.

The coast of South Carolina was laced with countless sandy islands, their beaches stretching like strands of hemp between earth and sky. Twisted oaks were dwarfed here and there by gangling palmetto trees.

At dawn on the morning of June 3 the sun shone through broken clouds and, as the morning wore on, the temperature rose and the officers gathered under the awning on the quarterdeck of the *De Molay*. At ten o'clock, the sailing ships of the blockading fleet came into view and soon Fort Sumter was sighted. Beyond Sumter, looking up the main ship channel and across the bright waters of the harbor, Shaw could see the roofs and spires of Charleston. At the wharves, along the north shore of the peninsula, the masts and shrouds of merchant ships traced a delicate pattern against the sky.

Gray packets still slipped into Charleston, under cover of darkness, bringing cargoes from Bermuda and Nassau, but most runners of the Federal blockade headed for Cape Fear now.

The *De Molay* was making its way south to Hilton Head Island where Shaw would report to General Hunter. Here the Fifty-Fourth would become part of a department whose main objective was the city of Charleston.

In 1861, Lincoln had decided to take the war to the place of its birth. A base of supplies was needed for the ships of the blockade, and footholds were needed for military operations against Charleston. At nine o'clock on the clear, cold morning of November 5, 1861, a great Federal armada, under the command of Commodore Francis Du Pont, had crossed the bar at Port Royal Inlet and reduced the forts and batteries on the islands of the archipelago. Du Pont's expedition had been a brilliant success in spite of accurate Confederate intelligence.

Now, in mid-1863, the Federals had as yet no foothold on the mainland, but other islands had fallen easily. The town of Beaufort, on Port Royal Island, was in Federal hands and there were soldiers and supplies on St. Helena Island, just across the inlet from Hilton Head. A year ago, attempts had been made to take Charleston but these had failed. At the moment, Federal regiments in the islands were not engaged. There had been raids on the mainland by the venerable First South Carolina Volunteers, now under the command of Colonel Thomas Wentworth Higginson, and by the growing Second South Carolina Volunteers under Colonel James Montgomery. But there had been no battles of moment since the late attempt to advance toward Charleston by way of contiguous James Island.

As the voyage drew to a close, the men busied themselves on the open decks rolling blankets, packing knapsacks and writing letters. Shaw wrote to his wife and said, with a tinge of homesickness, that it might be some time before they would find themselves, "driving about Berkshire together again." He wrote with pride of the passage of the regiment through Boston. "Just remember our own doubts and fears, and other people's sneering and pitying remarks when we began last winter, and then look at the perfect triumph of last Thursday. We have gone quietly along, forming the regiment, and at last left Boston amidst a greater enthusiasm than has been seen since the first three-months troops[1] left for the war." Shaw closed his letter with a tender, solicitous note advising her to "go to bed early, and take as much exercise as you can. . . ."

About two o'clock, the *De Molay* slid into Port Royal Inlet and threaded her way through some seventy ships whose masts and funnels broke the horizon above the flat, sun-flecked waters. She passed close to the frigates *Wabash* and *Vermont*, a couple of gunboats and a steamer flying the flag of France and docked at 2:30 at the end of a long pier which ran across the deeper water and shallows to the beach, where the roofs of the warehouses and sheds, built just after the occupation, reflected the sun. Shaw disembarked and walked beside the narrow gauge railroad track that ran the length of the pier. He passed the sheds and went straight to the high, white plantation house where General Hunter lived and worked. Hunter had a blunt face and long mustaches. His wife lived with him on Hilton Head and gossip had it that she was a better shot than he.

---

[1] Men who had enlisted for three months only.

Hunter had been an intimate of Lincoln, having accompanied the President-elect part way to Washington on his inaugural trip. Hunter had not completed the trip because of an injury to his collarbone but had gone on later and taken command of the White House Guard, spending his nights in the East Room. He had had the unpleasant duty of relieving the firmly rooted Frémont of his command of the Western Department, had taken command of the small and less important Department of the South in March of the previous year and, shortly thereafter, had captured Fort Pulaski in Georgia. This was no act of brilliance. Fort Pulaski had been lightly garrisoned. On April 13, 1861, shortly after the capture of Pulaski, Hunter had issued a statement declaring that "all persons of color lately held to involuntary service by enemies of the United States in Fort Pulaski and on Cockspur Island, Georgia, are hereby confiscated and declared free, in conformity with law, and shall hereafter receive the fruits of their own labor." Twelve days later, Hunter had put the three Southern states, parts of which were under his control, under martial law. On May 8, extending his proclamation, Hunter declared, "Slavery and martial law in a free country are altogether incompatible. . . . The persons in these three states, Georgia, Florida, and South Carolina, heretofore held as slaves are therefore declared forever free."

This decree had been unequivocally disavowed by Lincoln on the grounds that Hunter had exceeded his authority and had acted without informing his Commander-in-Chief.[2] In spite of his old friend's independence, Lincoln left Hunter leeway where the arming of blacks was concerned. After all, Hunter's predecessor, Thomas W. Sherman, had had authority to arm the slaves if "special circumstances require it." Unfortunately, Hunter, in his recruitment of contrabands, had allowed his officers to take Negroes straight from their work in the cotton fields, giving the men no chance to say good-by to their families and not making it clear that they would be paid and given furloughs from their regiments. Indeed, Hunter had some trouble getting Stanton to agree to pay the contrabands and altogether he was playing fast and loose with everyone involved—though, for a time at least, he was the darling of the North-

---

[2] John Charles Frémont had been slapped down by Lincoln in similar fashion after issuing his premature "emancipation proclamation" on August 30, 1861.

ern "radicals." Thomas Wentworth Higginson remembered later that Hunter's unfortunate handling of the recruitment of contrabands was never quite forgotten by men in the First South Carolina Volunteers, the ones who had had a brush with his methods.

As Shaw arrived, Hunter was being criticized for giving too much leeway to men like jayhawker James Montgomery and he was losing the respect of his officers. Shaw reported to Hunter that, with the exception of seasickness among his men the second and third days out and a narrow escape from grounding on Point Lookout shoals, the trip down had been uneventful. He emphasized that he would like to see his regiment put into service as soon as possible. Shaw wasn't much impressed by Hunter. He wrote, "There is some talk of his being removed."

Hunter boarded the *De Molay* with Shaw to inspect the troops and, later that day, wrote Governor Andrew, "From the appearance of the men I doubt not that this command will yet win a reputation and place in history deserving the patronage you have given them." He promised that the Fifty-Fourth would soon be "profitably and honorably employed."

Hunter ordered the regiment to Beaufort and, at four o'clock, the *De Molay* moved into the stream again and made her way upriver, passing Parris Island, rounding a bend and mooring off Beaufort just before dark. Early next morning, while the town slept, Shaw landed his men, marching them through the streets of the old town. Beaufort was a place of great charm. Sandy streets ranged around the curving waterfront, crossing each other at right angles. The streets and lawns were deep in the shade of spreading oaks, dripping with bluish Spanish moss. Stately white houses and beautiful gardens skirted a shell road that ran along the bluffs. Plantations on Port Royal had been seized as "abandoned lands" and parts of them sold by the United States government. The land the government retained was used for Treasury Department projects. The houses of the town were occupied by soldiers, government-employed civilians and former slaves. Many of the buildings in Beaufort had been built in colonial times. There was an arsenal, headquarters of the Beaufort Volunteer Artillery, organized in 1776. In the center of town was a spacious green.

In one of the fields of unworked plantation outside of town, the Fifty-Fourth made its bivouac. Here the men took shelter from the sun in the shade of bushes which had sprung up since the field had been worked.

T. W. Higginson's and Montgomery's regiments were in camp on Port Royal when Shaw arrived. Montgomery had just returned from what he described as a "successful foray up the Combahee River" bringing with him hundreds of contrabands who would be drafted into his regiment. Beside Negro units, the island was host to several other infantry regiments and a couple of encampments of cavalry and artillery. The landward side of the island, facing Confederate-held territory, was strongly fortified and heavily picketed.

Ned Hallowell's horse had died at sea and had been consigned to the deep, but Shaw lent Hallowell one of his horses and the two men rode into town to have a look around. On one of the streets they met Thomas Wentworth Higginson who had looked forward with great interest to the arrival of the Fifty-Fourth. He was an old friend of Governor Andrew and he felt that his reports to Andrew on the progress of his own regiment had helped Andrew prepare the way for the first Negro regiment raised in the North. Higginson was a tall, slightly awkward man of thirty-nine. Shaw invited him to share their first meal in camp. Higginson inspired a certain amount of awe in Shaw. The elder man was a man of letters as well as a soldier and Abolitionist. Shaw said of him, "I never saw one who put his whole heart into his work as he does; I was very much impressed with his open-heartedness and purity of character."

Higginson remembered that Shaw created a strong impression of "quiet power" and that "there was a tinge of watchful anxiety in his look."

The three officers talked about the singular problems confronting commanders of Negro soldiers. About six years later, Higginson wrote of the encounter in his *Army Life in a Black Regiment,* "I should have known Shaw anywhere by his resemblance to his kindred, nor did it take long to perceive that he shared their habitual truthfulness and courage. Moreover, he and Hallowell had already got beyond the commonplaces of inexperience, in regard to colored troops and, for a wonder, asked only sensible questions. For instance he admitted the matter of courage to be settled, as regarded the colored troops, and his whole solicitude bore on this point,—would they do as well in line-of-battle as they had already done in more irregular service, and on picket and guard duty? Of this I had, of course, no doubt, nor, I think, had he; though I remember his saying something about the possibility of putting them between two fires in case of need, and so cutting off their retreat. I should never have thought of such a project, but I could not have expected him to trust them as I did, until he had actually been under fire with them. That, doubtless, removed all his anxieties, if he really had any."

It was not uncommon, in the Civil War, and for that matter in more recent wars, for commanders to put their troops of whatever race "between two fires." But such an action would have been uncharacteristic of Shaw. He never wrote of or acted on such an impulse and there is no record of his mentioning "such a project" to anyone else.

A day or so later, Shaw met Colonel James Montgomery, now a spare, bearded man in his late forties. Montgomery was about to embark on another expedition to the coast of Georgia and Shaw, anxious that his men be put into action, asked him if they might go along. At first, Shaw liked Montgomery with his quiet voice and gentle manner. But he knew that this jayhawker's methods of achieving his ends had been anything but gentle. After the interview, Shaw wrote to his wife, "The bushwhacker Montgomery is a strange compound; he allows no swearing or drinking in his regiment, and is *anti-tobacco*: but he burns and destroys wherever he goes with great gusto, and looks as if he would have quite a taste for hanging people, whenever a suitable subject should offer." Shaw noted later that in spite of his bewitching charm, Montgomery's face had a rather fierce expression. He had a "queer roll or glare in his eye."

Since Montgomery's regiment was ready to sail, it was decided that Shaw would seek Hunter's approval and follow as soon as he could. Shaw had misgivings about putting himself under Montgomery's command. He wrote, "He is like an Indian in his mode of warfare, and, though I am glad to see something of it, I can't say I like it. It isn't like a fair stand-up fight, such as our Potomac army is accustomed to."

14.

At sunrise on June 8, after a rainy night, the Fifty-Fourth broke camp and marched through Beaufort to board the familiar *De Molay*. As the men waited on the decks of the transport, the sun rose above the river and the islands and salt marshes to the east. They waited in the growing heat until nine o'clock when the transport swung into the stream and ran down river. The men lined the rails in high spirits, talking and joking and singing songs. After a stop at Hilton Head, where Shaw reported again to Hunter and took on supplies, they steamed south along the coast toward St. Simons Island, running into a stiff breeze as darkness closed on the ship.

Early the following morning the transport dropped anchor on the inland shore near the southern point of St. Simons, at the mouth of the river that separated the island from the mainland. The northern reaches of the river were too shallow for navigation. At dawn, Shaw was rowed ashore on choppy waters. In the early light the island was mysterious and inviting, its white beaches fringed with cypress, stunted oak and thin, tousle-headed palmetto trees. The dark shapes of the trees were broken here and there by the flicker of the wings of a bright-colored bird. The islands' rivers were infested with alligators, and the mossy undergrowth was host to countless land and water snakes.

Shaw was put ashore and escorted to Montgomery's camp near Frederica. It was decided that the two men would bivouac on an abandoned plantation at Pike's Bluff, just south of the Butler estate and a few miles upriver. A shallow draft steamer came alongside the *De Molay* and, in a couple of trips, took the regiment up the murky waters. Shaw and Hallowell set themselves up in a poorly constructed plantation house and his men made camp on the edge of a field adjoining the house.

St. Simons had a colorful history. Near the camp at Pike's Bluff were the "tabby" walls of Frederica, founded by Governor Oglethorpe founder of Georgia in 1736. There John Wesley had preached, and in St. Simons "Bloody Swamp" invading Spaniards had been defeated in 1742. The Spanish force had contained a regiment of Negroes and one of mulattoes. During the American Revolution the island had been occupied by British troops and, early in the Civil War, had been fortified by the Secessionists, but in February of 1862 the armament had been removed.

The place had a special meaning for Shaw. They were close to the Butler plantation, parts of which were on St. Simon's and parts on other islands in the estuary of the Altamaha, including Butler Island a few miles northeast. While in Georgia, Fanny Kemble had come to know every corner of her husband's plantation and had known most of Pierce Butler's slaves. Writing from Butler Island during the early days of her residence, she had described St. Simons as being "between this savage selvage of civilization and the great Atlantic deep." Riding alone on St. Simons, she had noted that "every stump is a classical altar to the silvan gods, garlanded with flowers; every post, or stick, or slight stem, like Bacchante's thyrsus, twined with wreaths of ivy and wild vine, waving in the tepid wind. Beautiful butterflies flicker like flying flowers among the bushes, and the gorgeous birds, like winged jewels, dart from the boughs, and—and—a huge ground snake slid like a dark ribbon across the path while I was stopping to enjoy all this deliciousness. . . ."

Shaw remembered Fanny Kemble's stories about the Butler plantation. He commented, "I little thought that I should visit the place under such circumstances."

Shaw and Montgomery were very different. Shaw had a more objective view of the war. During his service with the Army of the Potomac, Shaw had developed no hatred of his enemy. In a letter from Front Royal, he had expressed a sentiment about his antagonists, a sentiment common to many a soldier before his time and since. "We have a very pleasant feeling toward the Rebel soldiers now. . . ." Fighting with Montgomery would be a different matter. Somewhere along the line, Montgomery had developed a virulent hatred of the aristocratic Southerners whose lush plantations laced the coastal plains and islands. The jayhawker was a man of limited intelligence and limited vision. He was impulsive and given to devising tactics at a moment's notice. Montgomery had been an intimate of John Brown and, despite his differences with the fabled man, had taken to Brown's methods like a duck to water. Montgomery had owned slaves himself when in Kentucky and had some firm ideas about dealing with blacks. In 1852, with his second wife, he had emigrated to the Midwest where he had purchased a claim at Mound City in Linn County, Kansas. Proslavery settlers had been in the majority in the southeastern part of the territory and Montgomery, in a country where lines were clearly drawn, had shortly become an Abolitionist, commanding a company of free-state men which had driven slave-owners out of Linn County and made predatory raids into Missouri. As Colonel of the Third Kansas Volunteers he had made a reputation as a plunderer. In 1862, after differences with General James H. Lane, Montgomery had gone to Washington to ask for authorization to raise his contraband regiment. Before Shaw's arrival at Port Royal Montgomery had accomplished several things of minor importance including the destruction of a railroad span over Buffalo Creek, a few miles west of Brunswick, Georgia.

Montgomery's recent raid up the Combahee, though it had bagged slaves for his regiment, had been marked by an excess of vandalism. A delayed dispatch to the *New York Daily Tribune* described the raid in these terms: "The soldiers scattered in every direction, and burned and destroyed everything of value they came across. Thirty-four large mansions known to belong to notorious rebels, with their rich furniture and rare works of art were burned to the ground. Nothing but smoldering ruins and crisped skeletons of once magnificent old oak and palmetto groves now remain of the delightful country seats."

Since the *Tribune's* dispatch was printed on June 10, Shaw couldn't have seen it, but he knew enough to make him uneasy.

On the following afternoon, June 10, a small steamer came up the river and docked at the rickety wharf. From her deck, Montgomery hailed Shaw. "How soon can you be ready to start on an expedition?"

Shaw answered, "In half an hour."

Montgomery's steamer left the wharf and soon disappeared around a bend in the river. Shaw ordered his drummer to sound the long roll. Before sundown, eight of Shaw's companies embarked on the shallow draft transport and steamed down river to Montgomery's camp, two companies staying behind to act as camp guards.

The Fifty-Fourth was joined by another transport carrying five companies of Montgomery's regiment and one section of Light Battery C., Third Rhode Island Artillery.

The transports ran hard aground near the mouth of the river, and there was a long delay while the captains of the ships waited for the flood tide. At one o'clock the next morning the ships floated free, looped around the southern tip of the island and steamed north while the passengers slept. At dawn they arrived in Doboy Sound, just north of Altamaha Sound, where they were joined by the gunboats *Harriet A. Weed* and *Paul Jones.*

The day was hot and clear and a few Confederate pickets, posted on a bluff overlooking the Altamaha, scanned the waters of the vast Atlantic, their faces in the shadow of the broad brims of their slouch hats. About mid-morning, they noticed a flotilla of four Federal ships north of their position. The ships were steaming south along the coast. At first the Confederates assumed that the flotilla would continue on its southerly course, but they watched intently until the shapes of the vessels grew more distinct above the sparkling water. Now, to the pickets' astonishment and alarm, the flotilla turned into Altamaha Sound, and they guessed that this might be more than a token raid. The appearance of a force of this size made it seem likely that the Federals were planning an excursion into the hinterland. The pickets rode to give the alarm to the commander of a detachment of the Twentieth Georgia Cavalry in the vicinity of Darien, nine or ten miles up the Altamaha from the mouth of the sound.

Shaw watched from the deck of his transport as the Federal flotilla moved upstream. On Montgomery's orders, his armed transport and gunboats shelled houses and clumps of trees as they went, but there was no answering fire. Not so much as a pea-shooter was directed against the Yankee ships. Shaw thought the shelling very brutal since Montgomery couldn't have known "how many women and children might be there." In fact, several weeks before, in anticipation of Federal bombardment and raids, most of the people of Darien had moved to a place called the Ridge, a few miles above the town and all but a handful of contrabands had fled when the pickets had spread the alarm. Elements of the Georgia cavalry regiment were now deployed along the river road between Darien and the Ridge.

Darien was a beautiful town built on a bluff high above the river.

The windows of its houses looked out to sea. Like Frederica, its site had been chosen by Governor Oglethorpe. It had been settled by Scottish highlanders from Inverness. It had become the financial center of Georgia, having been the home of the bank of Darien which had had branches throughout the state. During the Civil War, it was a point of departure for cargo vessels. A broad main street extended above and parallel to the river. There were other streets running into the main street at right angles. The streets were shaded by beautiful oak and mulberry trees that spread their branches over the houses. There were storehouses and a number of mills along the river bank and seventy-five to a hundred homes, many of them built in colonial times, their interiors graceful, the beams hand-hewn, the floors of fine, broad planks, their white walls holding paintings and tapestries, the handiwork of people of a bygone age. There were three churches in Darien, a market house, now bare of produce, a jail, courthouse and school and a steam sawmill owned by Yankee partners named Collins and Shine.

The Federal vessels moved up to the deserted wharves and the lines were secured to the creaking pilings. The soldiers made their way, sweating and slipping up the sandy paths that slanted along the bluff. The brigade formed in the public square while pickets were dispatched to look things over. Montgomery talked to Shaw in his quiet, unhurried way, telling him to order his men to remove all things of value from the houses and other buildings. The plunder would be taken down to the ships. Shaw questioned the breadth of the order, but Montgomery asserted that he was acting under orders from General Hunter. Two days before, Hunter had written Montgomery, issuing instructions that were quite specific. These had been based on General Order 100—"Instructions for the Government of Armies of the United States in the Field"—written by Francis Lieber. Hunter had asked that the enemy be given no basis for charging atrocities to the United States government—that Montgomery restrict himself to the acquisition of property which would be useful to the enemy in the pursuance of the rebellion, that he receive and enroll all able-bodied male fugitives who came within the Federal line, that he seize all food, including animals on the hoof. Anything was to be seized "which can be of service to our forces." Hunter had written that Montgomery would be justified in ordering the destruction of stores of grain and produce which could not be carried off. Hunter had added one restraining note. "All household furniture, libraries, churches, and hospitals you will of course spare." Shaw didn't see these instructions until several days after the raid.

Montgomery allowed his contrabands to break ranks and loot at will. But Shaw, sensing trouble, let his men leave the ranks only in the company of an officer and gave his officers instructions to take only things that might be useful in camp. Montgomery's soldiers, not accustomed to the refinements of civilization and not so well disciplined as Shaw's men, took a fancy to the looting like children running riot on Halloween. There was a holiday spirit as the soldiers broke ranks and fanned out into the streets and byways. Houses were entered or broken into, and unbridled foraging was started.

The men came back to the square on their way to the wharves like overloaded peddlers, carrying furniture and other personal belongings. Two men struggled with a spinnet piano, some carried mirrors and paintings, others brought bedspreads and assortments of tools. Books of all kinds were taken from the dwellings. Some of the soldiers went down to the ships with squawking chickens held by the feet. Cows were led through the streets by lengths of rope and torn sheets.

Shaw watched the looting in dismay, but there was little he could do to change the character of the raid. Montgomery commanded the expedition and had said that he was acting under orders. And, even if he was not, he did things by his own lights. Shaw wrote that Montgomery was impatient with what he called "the red tape way of doing things."

During the looting, the Mayor of Darien who had, some time before, removed himself to a house about three miles north of town, approached Darien in a buggy to see what was going on. He reined in on a knob of land about a mile from town. When he found no soldiers resisting the raid, he turned back and drove home where he saw some Confederate soldiers near his house. He told them they should be where the enemy was and said that if he had been commanding them he would certainly have ordered them to fire on the enemy. One of the pickets said that he wished the Mayor *had* been commanding them.

Materials of military value were taken from the warehouses

along the waterfront. Lumber, resin, grain, salt pork and other food-stuffs filled the holds of the Yankee ships. When the last of the stragglers had taken their loot to the ships, the soldiers formed again in the public square. Montgomery stood a few feet from Shaw. Suddenly he turned and said in a gentle voice, "I shall burn this town."

Shaw was thunderstruck. He had seen enough wanton behavior for one day. It was unthinkable that they should fire the town. He told Montgomery sternly that he would take no part in such an act. Montgomery said that he felt justified in doing such things because black regiments had been outlawed by the Confederates. Montgomery told Shaw, "The Southerners must be made to feel that this is a real war . . . that they will be swept away by the hand of God like the Jews of old."

But Shaw had no taste for becoming an instrument of the Lord. He refused to take a hand in this satanic action. One company of Shaw's men assisted in burning the town because Montgomery "ordered them out." Those who assisted, knowing their commander was opposed to the burning, went about it with little gusto. Most of Shaw's troops stood by with him in the public square while Montgomery went out to supervise the job.

During the morning a stiff breeze had sprung up. Barrels of turpentine were poured on the cotton, wheat and lumber that had not been carted off. When the warehouses burned, the smoke and flame could be seen for miles around. The men of the Fifty-Fourth's two companies that had been left behind as camp guards saw the smoke clearly from St. Simons and wondered what their brothers had gotten into.

The houses of Darien were reentered and turpentine was poured on the floors and lit with lucifer matches. Now the holiday air changed to one of grim, destructive orgy. Men ran yelling through the shimmering streets, torches held high, looking for unfired timber. It seemed that everything made by the hand of man was put to the torch. The remaining cows and calves bolted their confines and were shot down in the streets. Some slaves were taken to the ships but an old Negro woman named Nancy, who had come from Africa many years before, stoutly refused. The memory of her first sea voyage must have been unpleasant, at best. She just wouldn't go again on the "big water." Her captors let Nancy go and she left the town. Another woman was presented to Montgomery. Her skirt had been torn by grapeshot as the Yankee soldiers had fired on the town. Montgomery, as was his custom, spoke softly, telling her that her house would be spared, but he made no effort to keep his promise. Her house was burned.

In their headlong rush to fire the town, Montgomery's men burned churches and public buildings as well as houses. A "white" Methodist church failed to go up though it was fired in two places and a Negro Methodist church, a free Negro's cabin and several small houses were spared. The courthouse with all its records, the academy and Episcopal church were burned. The sawmill of Collins and Shine was entered but not fired. In the sawmill, one soldier wrote some of the names of the raiding party on one of the pages of an old ledger. Prominent on the list was the name of Robert Gould Shaw. This would create the false impression that Shaw had commanded the expedition.

Now the town was a crackling pillar of fire. Blackened chimneys and emaciated rafters stood against the orange flames. Great columns of smoke billowed upward, slanting with the wind as they blew away, thinning in the distance. Montgomery himself put the torch to the last building in the square and everyone scurried for the waterfront.

While the pillage had been in progress, the *Paul Jones* had made her way up the river with a detachment of soldiers who had found a large flatboat and the copper-bottomed schooner *Pet* about four miles above Darien. The *Pet* had been about to sail for the Bahamas and she held eighty bales of long staple cotton, worth about $30,000. The flatboat had carried five more bales. The men had seized the cotton and spared the schooner and the barge.

The *Paul Jones* returned to find the Darien waterfront a solid sheet of flame, Montgomery's and Shaw's troops scrambling down the sandy bluffs and boarding the transports to escape the heat of the withering buildings. When the men on the transports saw the *Paul Jones* moving toward them down the fiery river, they broke into wild cheers. The barrels of the ship's guns were so hot that the gunners were told to aim them at the sky. A change in the wind would have fired the ships at the wharves, and the magazines of the gunboats would have blown the flotilla to kingdom come. But the raiders were lucky. The *Paul Jones* passed the transports and was soon clear of danger. The lines of the other three ships were cast off and the flotilla moved away from the fury of the blaze.

15.

Shaw reached the camp at Pike's Bluff at 2 P.M. the day after the raid. He wrote first to his wife, giving her an account of the action. He said he felt that the raid was "as abominable a job" as he had ever had a share in. He cautioned her, "now dear Annie, remember not to breathe a word of what I have written about this raid, to anyone out of our two families, for I have not yet made up my mind what I ought to do."

Shaw felt that this kind of campaigning would "harm very much the reputation of black troops and those connected with them." He wrote, "I have gone through the war without dishonour, and I do not like to degenerate into a plunderer and a robber, and the same applies to every officer in my regiment. There was not a deed performed from beginning to end, which required any pluck or courage." Then, out of the depths of his discomfort, he wrote, "But all I complain of is wanton destruction. After going through hard campaigning and hard fighting in Virginia, this makes me very much ashamed of myself."

Montgomery was a restless man. He never lay quiet for more than a few days at a time and Shaw saw only two courses open to him—"to obey orders and say nothing; or refuse to go on any more such expeditions, and be put under arrest, probably court martialled, which is a serious thing."

It took very little thinking to bring Shaw to the conclusion that he would refuse to obey Montgomery's orders unless he was shown that they came from General Hunter. On the fourteenth, Shaw wrote to Lieutenant Colonel Halpine, the acting Adjutant General of the department, asking if Montgomery had orders to burn and destroy. On the same day he wrote a letter to Governor Andrew. He said in part, "On the 10th and 11th inst. we took part in an expedition under Colonel Montgomery. We met no enemy, and our only exploit was the capture of eighty-five bales of cotton and the burning of the town of Darien. The latter performance disgusted me exceedingly. I never knew before of a town being burnt to the ground without some good reason. . . . It seems to me that such a course is sure to bring discredit on the coloured troops if persisted in. The men themselves behaved very well. They plundered and destroyed only by order of the commanding officer. . . . Not a shot was fired at us from Darien. As far as I could ascertain, it is not a place of refuge for the rebels, and as our boats could at any time pass by it, up the Althamaha, the destruction seemed to me perfectly useless if not barbarous."

When the news of the raid reached Shaw's friends and family in the North, as it was bound to do, there was shock and disillusion that a regiment raised with so high a purpose should have taken part in such activity. Charles Lowell wrote Shaw's sister expressing his disappointment and wrote to William Whiting, solicitor of the War Department, on behalf of Shaw. "If burning and pillaging is to be the work of our black regiments, no first-rate officers will be found to accept promotion in them,—it is not war, it is piracy. . . ."

Lincoln heard about the raid and he didn't like it. It was the last in a series of straws that would break the back of the President's patience.

Hunter, protesting, was removed soon after. Lincoln, who was capable of writing and speaking plainly, answered Hunter's protestations with a masterful display of double talk. He wrote that the change in commanders was made "for no reasons which convey any imputation upon your known energy, efficiency and patriotism; but for causes which seemed sufficient, while they were in no degree incompatible with the respect and esteem in which I have always held you as a man and officer."

Shaw took lonely rides about St. Simons. The island was traversed from end to end by a shell road, making travel possible and even pleasant. Some sections of the highway were deep in the shade of overhanging trees while other parts were white and sunbaked, running through open country which was covered with sago palm, whose sharp, pointed leaves made the ground at the sides of the road impassable.

Except for abandoned slaves, living now in primitive conditions, the island had been "uninhabited for so long that it was completely full of birds of all kinds." Deer abounded on neighboring islands.

At one plantation, Shaw found the records of a "yacht race club and other signs of fun." Not far from camp, he discovered a beautiful little chapel, almost buried in trees and moss. Shaw saw to it that the building was "put to rights," and the first Sunday after the raid Montgomery's chaplain held services there.

Shaw, having a particular interest in a former resident of Pierce Butler's plantation, paid a visit to the place. He found "parts of it very beautiful," and in an abandoned plantation house he came upon a handful of Butler's slaves who remembered the "weeping day" when Butler had sold off members of their family at public auction.

The auction had taken place in 1859. A reporter for the *New York Daily Tribune* had written that "436 men, women and children and infants" had been sold. Old Major Butler had died, leaving the estate to his sons, and Pierce, having sustained losses in the crash of 1857–1858 and having gambled his way into debt, had decided to break up the family estate and "realize on his southern investments."

The *Tribune* had described the "negro speculators" as being a rough lot of men from the "back river and swamp plantations, where the elegancies of polite life are not perhaps developed to their fullest extent." These men from Georgia, the Carolinas, Alabama and Louisiana had been described as "bearish and profane."

A Negro without trade had sold for about $900 while a passable blacksmith or cooper went for $1600 or $1700. As was customary at slave auctions, families had been split up. There had been an air of finality about the tearful partings. Most of the Negroes who were sold had no idea where they were going and few could read or write. Mothers bid their children a last good-by. The departing slaves carried no more than the clothes they wore, perhaps an old slouch hat, a bright but tattered shirt and a patched skirt or pair of trousers. Few were shod. As they gathered in pathetic little knots with their new masters, Butler had made his rounds, giving each a silver dollar as a farewell gift.

The slaves were pleased to hear that Shaw knew "Miss Fanny" and asked if he could bring the children back. Shaw was saddened by the stories of hardship and loss but saw the empty houses as harbingers of freedom for the slaves. He wrote that "every lover of his country, even if he have no feeling for the slaves themselves, should rejoice."

The island's Circean wiles didn't hold Shaw spellbound very long. To pass the time, he and Hallowell hung a huge map of Georgia, taken at Darien, in the hall of the plantation house, "giving an air of solidity to the entrance." They lounged around listening to the buzzing of insects, swapping yarns or talking of home. By now, Shaw's brief round of marital bliss was a faraway dream. He read books on military tactics and Hallowell lay on his bed, staring at the ceiling, chanting the words of a mournful ditty that told of the feelings of all the men:

> No one to love, none to caress,
> None to respond to this heart's wretchedness.

Shaw wrote to his wife, "To-morrow is Sunday, and perhaps you will be at Staten Island; at any rate, I wish I could go to church with you, and saunter in some pretty garden afterwards."

Shaw was delighted with the news of Hunter's removal, thinking quite rightly that his successor would discourage Montgomery in his wanton destruction of private property. When Hunter was replaced by Brigadier General Quincy Adams Gillmore, Colonel Montgomery went alone to Hilton Head to report to his new commander. While he was absent, Shaw commanded the brigade.

On June 23, the *Harriet A. Weed* anchored off St. Simons, bringing Montgomery back with the news that Gillmore was planning an attack on the outlying defenses of Charleston. He would start with the capture of Morris Island at the gates of the harbor. Montgomery's brigade would be under the command of brilliant, thirty-year-old West Pointer, General George C. Strong.

On the brigade's first night aboard the transport *Den Bedford*, one of Montgomery's soldiers failed to obey an order to be silent after taps and the irrepressible jayhawker coolly drew his pistol and shot the man, wounding him. After the episode, Montgomery told Shaw that he had meant to kill his man and throw him into the sea. By now Shaw had seen enough of Montgomery to expect surprises, but he was "most amazed" that Montgomery had missed his aim.

St. Helena was swarming with Federal troops. Camps and supply dumps dotted the fields and lightly wooded plains close to the landing. St. Helena and Hilton Head were gathering places of most of the forces in Gillmore's department.

The Fifty-Fourth made camp in a pleasant place close to the sound where it was cool at night and the men could enjoy sea bathing.

St. Helena was the domain of the Port Royal Project, an attempt to utilize and educate the abandoned slaves who, like the few on St. Simons, lived in primitive conditions. In February of 1862, General Thomas W. Sherman, commanding the Port Royal area, had called for agents to operate the abandoned plantations and for teachers to instruct abandoned Negroes and their children. Able-bodied slaves were encouraged to work for the government for wages, producing cotton for the North. The missionaries of the project taught the illiterate to read and write and, as Sherman put it, familiarize themselves with the "rudiments of civilization and Christianity. . . ."

Shortly thereafter, the Port Royal area had been designated "the Department of the South" and put under the command of General Hunter. Edward L. Pierce, one of the speakers at the Joy Street church on February 16, had been appointed superintendent of the project. Pierce had been specifically ordered by the Administration to "prevent deterioration of the estates, secure their best civilization and promote the welfare of their laborers."

This, the first missionary expedition of its kind, was supported by the Treasury Department and was the darling of the antislavery workers.

The closing stanzas of a poem by Whittier, written for the teachers and schoolchildren on St. Helena, expressed the sentimental feelings that the Northerners had about the Port Royal experiment.

> The very oaks are greener clad,
> The waters brightly smile;
> Oh, never shone a day so glad,
> On sweet St. Helena Isle!
>
> For none in all the world before
> Were ever glad as we, ——
> We're free on Carolina's shore,
> We're all at home and free!

The Port Royal Project had the support of charitable organizations in Massachusetts, New York and Pennsylvania. At first, the Negroes' ignorance had given trouble. One woman had believed that the Yankees were horned beasts. But, despite this fear of the Yankee strangers and notwithstanding General Hunter's handling of the blacks, Gideon's Band—as the people of the mission were called—had by now gained the confidence of the Negroes.

In the fall of 1862, disenchanted with Hunter's recruiting methods, the Administration had sent Brigadier General Rufus Saxton to Port Royal with the title of military governor—it being understood that he was to carry forward the arming of blacks. Saxton had succeeded where Hunter had failed and was very popular with the Negroes. For reasons best known to Lincoln himself, Hunter, until now, had been kept on as commander of the department.

On the first Sunday in camp on St. Helena, the heavens were roiled by a series of violent thunderstorms. Tents were blown down and one man was killed by a bolt of lightning. On this storm-battered day, Montgomery added to his list of crimes. He caught a man in the act of deserting and ordered him shot without court-martial.

On the thirtieth, the Fifty-Fourth was mustered for pay and it was learned that the government would not adhere to the terms of enlistment. Shaw vented his anger in a letter to Governor Andrew. He said in part:

"You have probably seen the order from Washington which cuts down the pay of colored troops from $13 to $10. Of course if this affects Massachusetts regiments, it will be a great piece of injustice to them, as they were enlisted on the express understanding that they were to be on precisely the same footing as all other Massachusetts troops. In my opinion they should be mustered out of the service or receive the full pay which was promised them." Referring to the paymaster, Shaw said, "If he does not change his mind, I shall refuse to have the regiment paid until I hear from you on the subject." This Shaw did. The matter of pay would be a subject of discussion and a source of discontent among the men of the Fifty-Fourth until the regiment was disbanded.[1]

---

[1] After Shaw's death at Wagner, the fight over pay went on. Colonel Montgomery made an insulting speech to the Negro soldiers, trying to intimidate them. He addressed the heroes of the attack on Wagner in these terms, "you have not proved yourselves as soldiers. . . ." He asserted that he was a friend of the Negro. "I was the first person in the country to employ nigger soldiers in the United States Army. . . . I had a lot of niggers and a lot of mules; and you know a nigger and a mule go very well together."

But the men of the Fifty-Fourth still refused payment on the grounds that they were not "holding out for money" but "from principle." Sergeant Swails, of the Fifty-Fourth, while doing the work of the government in the field, learned that his family had been placed in the poorhouse. Emilio, the regimental historian, reported that other stories of hardship among the families of soldiers of the Fifty-Fourth would "fill a volume." Finally,

On the evening of July 2, Shaw paid a visit to a plantation not far from camp where he met eight teachers who had come to the islands to assist in the work of the Port Royal Project. One of these was Miss Charlotte Forten, a young and beautiful Negro woman whom Shaw described as a "quadroon."² Shaw was attracted to Charlotte Forten and he wrote that she was the "belle" of the sea islands. He found her a well-educated and interesting person. She was apparently quite smitten with Shaw. She wrote in her diary, "To me he seems a thoroughly lovable person." Later she wrote to his mother of "the singular charm of his manner, the nobleness of soul that shone through his face."

After tea at the plantation, Shaw went with the teachers to a "praise-meeting." He wrote, "The praying was done by an old, blind fellow, who made believe all the time that he was reading out of a book." The blind man led the singing too and he "seemed to throw his whole soul into it." After the meeting, they went to a "shout" where Shaw saw the shuffling in a ring, the singing, chanting and clapping still seen in some of the sea islands. Charlotte Forten wrote of Shaw, "We looked upon him with the deepest interest. There was something in his face finer, more exquisite than one often sees in a man's face, yet it was full of courage and decision. . . . How full of life and hope and lofty aspirations he was that night! How eagerly he expressed his wish that he might be ordered to Charleston." Indeed, Shaw was eager to go into action. A few days later he would write, "I want to get my men alongside white troops, into a good fight, if there is to be one."

July 4 was a bright, clear day and Shaw went with Charlotte Forten to the grounds of a Baptist church where the freedmen on the island gathered to hear a sermon by a Baltimore preacher, a Negro named Lynch. The crowd collected in the churchyard under

under prodding from a number of quarters, there was Congressional action. The Equalization Bill, as it was called, was reported on March 2, 1864. Senate committees wrangled for several months, and finally a version of the bill was passed. It contained the incredible provision that equal pay would be granted only to men who had been "free" since April 19, 1861. Colonel Edward Hallowell, then in command of the Fifty-Fourth, drafted an oath, masterful in its lack of definition, which all the men of the regiment, as well as the men of the Fifty-Fifth, were able to swear to.
² Charlotte Forten was a Negro and thought of herself as such. Her skin was lighter than that of many Negroes, but she was certainly not a "quadroon."

the oaks. "The gay dresses and turbans of the women made the sight very brilliant."

Shaw was enthusiastic about the results of the Port Royal experiment. He wrote his mother, "Can you imagine anything more wonderful than a colored abolitionist meeting on a South Carolina plantation? There were collected all the free slaves on this island, listening to the most ultra abolition speeches that could be made, while two years ago their masters were still here, the lords of the soil and of them. Now they all own something themselves, go to school and to church, and work for wages! It's the most extraordinary change. Such things oblige a man to believe that God is not very far off.

"A little black boy read the 'Declaration of Independence,' and then they all sang their hymns; the effect was grand. . . .

"Miss Forten promised me to write out the words of some of the hymns they sang, which I will send you."[3]

On the evening of July 6, Shaw, Hallowell and another officer entertained Miss Forten and two of her colleagues at camp. Some of Shaw's men sang for his guests and, after the entertainment, Shaw sat and chatted with Charlotte Forten. That night, before she retired, she took pen in hand and wrote in her diary, "Tonight he helped me on my horse, and after carefully arranging the folds of my riding skirt, said, so kindly, 'Goodbye, if I don't see you again down here, I hope to see you at our house.' "

Before Shaw retired, he had sterner things on his mind. Most of the commanders of regiments on the island had received orders to move to islands around Charleston, but to Shaw's bitter disappointment no orders had come for the Fifty-Fourth. That evening he wrote to Strong:

St. Helena Island, July 6, 1863.

Brig.—Gen. George C. Strong

General,—I did not pay my respects to you before you left this post because I did not wish to disturb you when making your preparations for departure.

I desire, however, to express to you my regret that my regiment no longer forms a part of the force under your command. I was the more disappointed at being left behind, that I had been given to understand that we were to have our share in the work of this

---

[3] After Shaw's death, Charlotte Forten kept her promise. She sent the words of the hymns to Shaw's mother.

department. I feel convinced too that my men are capable of better service than mere guerilla warfare, and I hoped to remain permanently under your command.

It seems to me quite important that the colored soldiers should be associated as much as possible with white troops, in order that they may have witnesses besides their own officers to what they are capable of doing. I trust that the present arrangement is not permanent.

With many wishes for your success, believe me very sincerely and respectfully

Your obediant servant,
ROBERT G. SHAW,
Colonel Commanding Fifty-Fourth Regiment Mass. Infantry.

On July 8, Shaw's fear of inactivity was dissolved by an order directing him to prepare to leave at an hour's notice. His men were to take only blankets, cold rations and battle equipment. In fact, by now, rations were in pitifully short supply. Shaw's men had little to pack but hardtack and dried bread.

Three hours after the order was received, Montgomery's brigade boarded the steamers *Chasseur* and *Cossack*. Shaw left two companies behind as camp guards.

16.

The sky above the islands was darkened by swiftly moving, leaden clouds. A thunderstorm was brewing in the east. The vast, gray waters of the Atlantic were flecked with white as the ships ploughed into the open sea. When she was more than a mile off shore, the *Chasseur*, carrying Shaw and most of his regiment, headed north, now followed by the *Cossack*, the bows of the transports crashing into the foaming waters. As the gray light of day gave way to the blackness of night, wind-whipped rain drenched the deserted decks of the ships.

Shaw and Hallowell had comfortable quarters but it was hard to sleep on the rolling ship. The steamer was small and very crowded, conditions made worse by the scarcity of food and water. Below decks it was hot and close. The men passed the early hours of the night in extreme discomfort, jammed into the foul-smelling holds and passageways, awash with the evidence that many had been sick.

The coastal islands of South Carolina were passed unseen by the helmsmen and officers on watch aboard the transports. The voyage from Port Royal Sound to Folly Island covered some forty miles in the open sea and it was nearly midnight when the ships arrived off Stono Inlet at the southern point of Folly Island. Shaw wrote to his wife, "We lay off the bar until 1 P.M. waiting for the flood-tide. The sea was running very high all the time. . . ."

Folly Island was a long, thin outer island which pointed northeast like a crooked finger, ending at Lighthouse Inlet which divided Folly from the southern end of Morris Island. Just north of Folly lay a lacy complex of rivers, salt marshes and creeks, surrounding countless smaller islands. North of these was James Island, bordered on the north by Charleston Harbor and Wappoo Creek which separated it from the mainland. James was larger than Morris or Folly and along its western shore ran the navigable Stono River which separated it from still larger John's Island.

Shaw's letter to Annie continued, "We then steamed up the Stono River in company with the Monitor 'Nantucket,' the gunboat 'Pawnee' and two other little gunboats and seven transports. . . .

"We now lie off the place where General Hunter's troops landed last year in the attack on Charleston. The sail up the river was beautiful, the sun just sinking as we reached our anchorage."

Stono Inlet was full of transports that day, all of them loaded to the rails with troops, all in plain view of the Confederate pickets on the nearby sand hills, their movements followed by the sentry in the tower of Charleston's St. Michael's Church.

Sailing up the river, the *Chasseur* and the other transports were led by gunboats which shelled John's Island on the left and James on the right. Thirteen transports passed up the Stono that afternoon, carrying Montgomery's brigade and two white brigades under Brigadier General Alfred Terry whose force would make a diversionary attack on James Island, the real objective being Morris Island.

Hunter's successor, General Gillmore, whose brilliant performances as a soldier and military engineer had rocketed him upward since the start of the war, had taken part in the engagement which had secured Hilton Head in 1861, then left the islands for commands in Kentucky and West Virginia.

Gillmore, his sights set on Charleston, had, as yet, no foothold on Morris Island. Morris Island was shaped like a pork chop, the thin, bony part curving around to the north toward Sumter. At the end of this narrow neck of land were four batteries, the largest of these being Battery Gregg. Gregg was at the northern tip of the island, its guns looking out to sea and across the mouth of the great harbor. South of these four batteries, guarding this strategic bit of sand from land assault, was Fort Wagner. Wagner was a gigantic earthwork, perhaps the strongest ever built. Its position was formidable. It stretched from the Atlantic on the east to the marshes of deep, meandering Vincent's Creek on the west and could only be approached by direct assault along a spit of sand, narrow even at low tide. An attacking force would face not only Wagner's guns but the guns of Sumter, James and Sullivan's Islands as well. Wagner's guns were so placed that an invader would face flanking fire as well as direct.

Possession of Wagner and the other Morris Island batteries, whose fall would inevitably follow Wagner's fall, would enable Gillmore to turn his own and abandoned Confederate guns against Fort Sumter which could then be reduced by siege. Sumter and the Morris Island batteries having been rendered ineffective, Admiral Dahlgren, now commanding the South Atlantic blockading squadron, could, it was thought, enter Charleston Harbor bombarding the other batteries and forts as he advanced.

While the diversionary force passed up the Stono, masked batteries were set up on the north tip of Folly Island, concealed from the enemy by a convenient growth of trees and bushes. Gillmore planned to launch his attack on Morrris Island from this point. Troops would be brought here under cover of darkness and sent across the inlet in small boats, made for the purpose of rough milled pine and primed over with lead and oil.

For his operations against Charleston, Gillmore was using most of the military potential of his department. He had plenty of men and weapons and a good supply of sundry equipment, but the Fifty-Fourth was not the only regiment in his command that lacked food. The shortage of food was widespread.

On the tenth, still writing from the transport *Chasseur*, now anchored in the Stono River by James Island, Shaw reported, "This afternoon I went inland about two miles, and from a housetop saw Fort Sumter, our monitors, and the spires of Charleston. Just now the news of the fall of Vicksburg, and of Lee's defeat, has reached us. What excitement there must be throughout the North! For my part though, I do not believe the end is coming yet, and the next mail will probably tell us that Lee has gotten away with a good part of his army. . . ."

Later that afternoon, still aboard the *Chasseur*, Shaw and his men heard heavy cannonading from the direction of Morris Island and, by sunset, they had word that Gillmore's attack had been a success. The Federals now held all the ground south of Wagner. They were poised for an attack against the sloping walls of the earthwork. The following morning, July 11, came the news of the repulse of the first attack against Wagner.

On James Island, Fort Pemberton, in front of the Wappoo River, was in the northwest corner and constituted the enemy's right. From Pemberton, the line ran roughly southeast, crossing flat marshland, low timber and country roads and ending at Secessionville. Secessionville was fronted by an earthwork called Battery Lamar. The Federal engineers on James were busy improving the line of land retreat. Bridges and causeways were repaired so that a march could be made to Cole's Island, one of the network of islands lying between James and Folly.

Montgomery's brigade landed and camped in the furrows of an unworked field where they made shelters against the merciless summer sun. Though the Fifty-Fourth was officially part of Montgomery's brigade, Shaw and the other regimental commanders took their orders directly from General Terry. Now Shaw was no longer accountable to Colonel Montgomery. For the first time, Shaw sent out pickets to serve with whites in other regiments. He wrote that his men had "no trouble with them."

For four days, Shaw's pickets saw very few Confederates. One of his companies retired under pressure and Shaw reported later that his men behaved well. He wrote, "The Rebel pickets call to us that they will give us three days to clear out.

"We have not had our clothes off since we left St. Helena, and have absolutely nothing but an India rubber blanket apiece. Officers and men are in the same boat."

On Wednesday, the fifteenth, Shaw had four companies out on picket. Captain Simkins, whose decision to serve in a Negro regiment had come as "the result of much hard thinking," occupied ground on the left. Simkins was a fine young officer, good-looking and solidly built, with a strong chin and a pleasant manner. He had deployed his men in a line running through light timber and brush. From Simkins's left to the Stono River, the line was continued by men of the Tenth Connecticut. The men of the Tenth held a dangerous position. They had a swamp in their rear and a breakthrough on their right, at Simkins's position, would cut them off.

There were frequent showers as darkness came on. Simkins's men and the men of the Tenth were uneasy as they strained their eyes to penetrate the gloom. Once in awhile a shot rang out. Just to the right of Simkins's position, Captain Willard of the Fifty-Fourth climbed to the roof of a deserted house and perched on the ridge pole. From this vantage point he could see a great bustle in the ranks of the Confederate signal corps. Willard passed the word to expect an attack.

In the gray light of dawn on the sixteenth, the enemy dropped a few shells behind Shaw's picket line. One of his officers clambered to the top of a pile of empty cracker boxes and, teetering there, saw flashes of musketry just beyond the trees along the line of enemy outposts. Then to the left came the sharp, metallic explosions of field guns, close to the Stono where the enemy had galloped a cluster of Napoleons into battery. A couple of shots crashed into the *Pawnee* killing some men and injuring others. Since the channel was too narrow for the gunboats to turn so their guns could bear on their tormentors, they couldn't answer the enemy fire.

Now Shaw's drummer sounded the long roll and his adjutant, Wilkie James,[1] rode along the line kicking his horse and shouting, "Fall in! Fall in!" Shaw cantered along the line, his unsheathed sword in his right hand, ordering the main body of the regiment into position to await an attack.

The first point of contact was at Simkins's position. There, enemy soldiers swept out of the gloom yelling shrilly, at first creating some confusion. Simkins coolly and swiftly rallied the men who were closest to him and the others stood their ground. The fighting was fierce as Simkins's men contested every inch of soil in their forced retreat. Again and again they faced the enemy, exposing themselves to withering fire, gaining time for the men of the Tenth to pull out of their cul-de-sac.

All along the line that morning, the Negroes of Shaw's picket line, in their first baptism of fire, displayed the bravery that Shaw had believed they would display.

First Sergeant Peter Vogelsang, a lantern-jawed Negro who sported a mustache, had taken his position by a palmetto tree. It seemed to him that at one moment he was waiting for action and in the next "one hundred Rebels were swarming about me." He led his men forward, firing as he went, and somehow escaped without a scratch.

There were men who refused to fall back, though no loss of honor was attached to retreat. Negro Sergeant James D. Wilson, who was known as the handsomest soldier in the regiment, had told his men that he would never retreat. Wilson was as good as his word. As the enemy swept toward him he shouted to his men to stand fast. His shouts attracted five charging Confederates who turned on him.

---

[1] Garth Wilkinson James, a brother of William and Henry James.

He disabled three and the others passed by. A detachment of cavalry moved toward Wilson out of the smoke and, yelling fiercely, he leaped at them as they circled around, keeping them at bay with the point of his bayonet. Finally, peppered with bullets, he pitched forward and lay still.

Captain Russel, a slight man with a hawklike nose who was defending ground on the right of the picket line, was charged by a mounted Confederate whose sword sang through the air as he tried to hit Russel in the head. Russel's life was saved by one of his men who leaped toward the horseman, catching the second sweep of his sword on his bayonet and shooting the Confederate through the neck.

The time gained by the stiff resistance of the pickets, especially those of the Fifty-Fourth, had enabled the main body of Terry's division, including Shaw and the soldiers of his regiment who were not on picket, to form a line. The pickets began to come in from the front. It seemed that the Confederate force would be in hot pursuit. Some of the retreating pickets limped along unassisted; others were supported by their comrades-in-arms. One Negro covered the ground steadily enough though his arm was shattered, his right sleeve tattered and covered with blood. Captain Russel, whose life had been saved by his sergeant's bayonet, struggled in supporting a Negro much bigger than himself. Simkins, who had saved the men of the Tenth Connecticut, brought up the rear. His trousers and rubber coat were riddled with holes, but the bullets had somehow missed the man.

Now Shaw, who expected an attack in force, was troubled by the silence that pervaded the place. The gunboats on the rivers should be giving them support. At last a welcome sound was heard. Parrot guns boomed. There was support from the right as well as the left, gunboats having run up Big Folly Creek during the night before. The Federal artillery fire was so heavy that the enemy failed to appear. Two companies of the Fifty-Fourth advanced skirmishing, and the main body followed under Shaw. As the men took up their old positions, it was clear that the fighting was over for the day.

While Shaw's regiment, as part of Terry's brigade, was engaged in their successful diversionary demonstration on James Island and Strong's brigade was securing ground on Morris Island preparatory to an attack on Fort Wagner, Colonel Thomas Wentworth Higginson with his Negro regiment, the First South Carolina Volunteers, was ordered to ascend the South Edisto River and destroy a bridge, cutting the line of the Charleston and Savannah Railroad at Jacksonborough in order to delay the arrival of reinforcements from Savannah. Of the three simultaneous operations, Higginson's alone was a signal failure. In his own account of the ascent of the Edisto, he wrote charmingly of the moonlit landscape as he started off on the evening of July 9. He wrote of encounters with terrified slaves. Higginson's boat, the *Enoch Dean*, was forced to turn back when it was two miles below his objective. The *Dean*'s machinery gave him trouble and Higginson, unfamiliar with the shallow channel, ordered the *Dean* to start downstream at the turning of the tide. His tug, which Higginson described as a "little mosquito," ran aground and Higginson was forced to order it burned. Two pieces of artillery, which had been thrown overboard to lighten the tug, were lost.

While Shaw's Negro soldiers had been rising to their first baptism of fire, the draft riots raged in the City of New York. Mercifully the mails to the islands were slow and the men in the department would not have news of the riots for days. Started as a peaceful protest of the underprivileged, mostly Irish, against an injustice in the draft law, which allowed a man who had three hundred dollars to hire a stand-in, riots had erupted in a flood of hate, developing into an orgy of rape, murder and wholesale arson directed mainly against the Negroes of the city. Negroes had been attacked by mobs and subjected to unprintable atrocities. Others had been hanged from lamp posts, chunks of flesh cut out of their bodies. The naked bodies of dead Negroes had been dragged through the streets, stoned and burned.

The New York Times reported that there was some evidence that Confederate agents "were using both energy and money in feeding the flames that have for three days darkened and three nights reddened the sky of New York."

After the fight on James Island, Shaw sent out parties to scour the ground for wounded and dead. Several wounded men were found lying in some brush near a creek and they were brought in. It looked as if some of the dead had been mutilated by the enemy, but close inspection showed that the work had been done by the fiddler crabs that flourished in the salt marshes of the coastal islands.

The body of a young Confederate soldier was carried in. He was, "almost a child, with soft skin and long fair hair, red with his own blood." Shaw's men dug a grave and buried the boy in the sandy soil.

Of the enemy's treatment of prisoners, Shaw wrote his wife, "We found some of our wounded, who say that the Rebels treated them kindly. Other men report that some prisoners were shot. It is very common for frightened men to tell fearful stories of what they have seen; the first report comes from the wounded themselves; the second from some stragglers."

Shaw's adjutant brought him a message from General Terry. "Tell your Colonel that I am exceedingly pleased with the conduct of your regiment." And a war correspondent for *The Reflector* reported, "The boys of the Tenth Connecticut could not help loving the men who saved them from destruction. I have been deeply affected at hearing this feeling expressed by officers and men of the Connecticut regiment; and probably a thousand homes from Windham to Fairfield have, in letters, been told the story of how the dark-skinned heroes fought the good fight and covered with their own brave hearts the retreat of brothers, sons and fathers of Connecticut."

Mail was received that afternoon. Hallowell wrote that he and Shaw "sat down together and read our letters, and then talked of our homes, and the friends we might never see again. During the conversation I asked him if, in case we charged the fort [Wagner], he intended to go in front of his men or behind them; to which he replied, 'I cannot tell now, but trust God will give me strength to do my duty.'"

Hallowell continued, "He then asked me if I believed in presentiments, and said he felt he should be killed in the first action. I told him I thought it wrong to yield to such a feeling, and he must shake it off."

Shaw answered, "I will try."

After he read his mail, Shaw wrote to his wife, giving her an account of the events of the morning. "All this is very gratifying to us personally, and a fine thing for our coloured troops. It is the first time they have been associated with white soldiers. . . .

"To make my happiness and satisfaction complete, the afternoon brought yours and Mother's letters."

Shaw closed, "Good bye, darling, for the night. I know this letter

will give you pleasure, because what we have done today wipes out
the memory of the Darien affair, which you could not but grieve
over, though we were innocent participators. . . ."

His purpose accomplished, General Terry was ordered to evacuate
James Island. At sunset the Fifty-Fourth retired to the landing. The
men were tired. Some talked of lost comrades, all spoke with pride
of their accomplishment.

The sky was black and thunder rumbled in the distance. Once in
a while a flash of lightning was seen in the east.

The Tenth Connecticut and Montgomery's brigade, including the
Fifty-Fourth, were ordered to return to the mouth of the Stono by
land while the other regiments boarded the transports. While the
soldiers waited for marching orders, the men of the Tenth, who had
been saved by Simkins's company, came over to offer their thanks
and shake hands all around.

As darkness fell, the burgeoning clouds spilled torrents of rain.
After dark the men who held the line began to withdraw, the withdrawal being accomplished so stealthily that enemy pickets were
none the wiser.

Shaw and some engineers who knew the terrain, led off on foot
and the three regiments marched into the darkness. Lightning
stabbed the sky again and again, and the wind drove the rain against
the men's faces. At first, the path was wide enough so the men
could march two abreast. The soles of their boots slapped a tired
tattoo on the sodden ground. A heavy wooden bridge was crossed
and destroyed. Now the path grew narrow and led across a series
of footbridges, in some places only one plank wide. Flashes of
lightning revealed the men, each clinging to the belt or folds of
the coat of the man ahead, as they struggled along the dipping
planks, supported by swaying, drunken pilings. Sometimes, passing
over swamps, the groping men skidded and plunged into water several feet deep, then hoisted themselves to the planks again, fetid
water cascading over the tops of their boots and dripping from their
clothes.

The rain drove downward through the night. The thunder added
an ominous note and the lightning deepened the following dark.
Now a footpath snaked through a swamp where the men's boots
gathered heavy clods of puttylike clay. They passed through timber

where wet branches cut their faces and hands. More swamps were entered and passed. Shaw computed their speed. "It took from 10 P.M. to 5 A.M. to come four miles."

By the time they reached firmer ground, the rain had subsided and the pink light of day was touching the sky above the sea. The first men, mud-covered, scratched and tattered, emerged from the swamp and threw themselves down on the muddy ground and slept until the regiment was brought together and formed again to resume the interrupted march. Now the ground improved and the men passed over a bridge that led to Cole's Island where they halted within sight of the broad Atlantic. The day was clear and the men slept until the rising sun flooded the landscape with brilliant light. The dunes grew crowded. Regiments had been arriving on Cole's Island not only from James but by transport from other points as well. Men lounged and dozed all along the stretch of sand, waiting for boats to take them across to Folly Island. As the sun reached its zenith, the glare on the sand was almost more than eyes could bear. The men were footsore and thirsty. There were no rations to be had. Shaw wrote to his wife, "There is hardly any water to be got here, and the sun is dazzling and roasting us. I shouldn't like you to see me as I am now; I haven't washed my face since day before yesterday. My conscience is perfectly clear about it though, for it is an impossibility and everyone is in the same condition. Open air dirt, I.E. mud, etc. is not like the indoor article. . . .

"We have had nothing but crackers and coffee these two days. It seems like old times in the army of the Potomac. Good-bye again, darling Annie."

The day of waiting passed slowly. Shaw talked to Hallowell about the work that lay ahead, watched the horizon for passing ships and dreamed of home and a time of peace. Early that evening, a moist, cool breeze blew across the islands, and at eight o'clock Shaw was brought the happy news that he was to report to General Strong. Strong had Shaw's letter of the sixth and he knew of the bravery of Shaw's pickets under attack. He was ready to give the Fifty-Fourth a chance to show what it could do in line of battle. Strong's order took Shaw out of Montgomery's command, since Montgomery wasn't ordered to report to Strong.

Shaw was told that the *General Hunter* was waiting closeby, ready to ferry his regiment to Folly Island. He marched the regiment to the shores of a broad creek where the *Hunter* was anchored in deep water. A single longboat would provide the only means of transferring the men from shore to transport.

With the suddenness of tropic change, another storm sent its billowing smudges across the night sky. Again, the rumble of thunder was heard. A mist moved along the tidal creek and the riding lights of the *General Hunter* winked weakly behind the milky veil. Shaw stood by as the longboat was loaded. There would only be room for thirty men a trip. Most of the men were close to exhaustion. The lack of adequate transportation would cost them another night of sleep.

Shaw watched the bobbing of the lonely lantern that lit his men to the decks of the *Hunter*. Word came from the transport that a cabin was waiting for Shaw if he chose to use it, but he stayed with his men as the storm broke, drenching them all. The men sat around in the low marsh grass, quietly talking, dozing and waking, waiting for their turns as Shaw brooded over the loading of the boat. The current was strong, the soldiers crowded the men at the oars. As the boat crossed the current, it rocked from side to side frightening the men who couldn't swim. First one end and then the other was sucked downstream. The bailing can was kept in play as the water was driven through the leaks.

Dawn approached and the rain subsided. As sunrise touched the dappled sky, Shaw climbed in with the last boatload of men, took the tiller and guided the longboat across the current.

17.

Shaw and Ned Hallowell stood on the deck of the *Hunter* with Captain Simkins and Captain Russel. Russel was in a talkative mood. Shaw listened for a few minutes, then wandered off. When Hallowell tired of the conversation he looked for Shaw and found him lying near the pilot house on the top deck. Hallowell asked, "Rob, don't you feel well? Why are you so sad?"

Shaw turned to Hallowell and said, "Oh Ned! If I could live a few weeks longer with my wife, and be home a little while I think I might die happy. But it cannot be. I do not believe I will live through our next fight."

The men stayed together without speaking. Then Shaw asked Hallowell to leave him alone—said he wanted to think about his home. Hallowell wrote, "In an hour he came down. All sadness had passed from his face, and he was perfectly cheerful. . . ."

The *Hunter* ran up Folly River, docked and disgorged the regiment which marched the length of the island, the Atlantic Ocean on their right and sand hillocks on the left. As they marched, they heard artillery fire straight ahead on Morris Island. White soldiers, in camps along their route of march, had heard of their work on James Island and called out words of praise and encouragement. When they reached Lighthouse Inlet, separating Folly from Morris Island, some of the men gathered around the regimental colors and broke into song. Some of the men on the sand found the strength to write to their loved ones at home. One of these was handsome First Sergeant Simmons, who had fought bravely on James Island. Simmons wrote to his mother in New York City. "We fought a desperate battle. . . ." Simmons wrote of the death of comrades. "God has protected me through this, my first fiery leaden trial, and I do give him the glory, and render praises unto His holy name."

Simmons closed with the words, "God bless you all! Goodbye! Likely we shall be engaged again soon. Your affectionate son, R. J. Simmons."

Three days earlier, unknown to Simmons, a tragedy had taken

place in his tenement home at 147 East Twenty-eighth Street in New York. By Wednesday, July 15, Simmons's mother, his sister Mrs. Susan Reed and his sister's two children, who lived together in the same rooms, had been thoroughly frightened by the riots in the streets, by the murder and rape. But they hadn't fled the city as many others had done or tried to do. One of Sergeant Simmons's sister's children was a babe-in-arms, the other a boy of seven years. The boy was described by the family pastor as a comely child, always punctual in his attendance at school, tidy in appearance, eager to learn. He was a cripple, though the nature of his handicap was not recorded.

On this fateful day, a mob entered Simmons's block, striking terror into Negro residents. Simmons's sister was a laundress. With incredible conscientiousness she took it into her head that the rioters might steal or damage a basket of laundry she had just finished ironing a short time before. She hurried to take the basket of clothes back to its owner, leaving her children in the care of her mother.

As the rioters came closer, Simmons's mother started off to take the children to a place of safety, but somehow the boy was separated from her and found himself in front of the house surrounded by men who set about beating him with sticks. He was struck several times with heavy stones torn by the men from the ragged pavement and finally attacked by a bitter-faced man and hit on the temple with the butt of a pistol.

A strapping young fireman named John F. McGovern, wearing the customary bright red shirt and black pants tucked into his boots, swept the child up, his eyes blazing in a frenzy of outrage, and stood off the mob with his free arm, menacing the men with his great fist. McGovern carried the wounded boy to the home of a woman who begged him on her knees to take the Negro boy away so she wouldn't have trouble with the mob. McGovern found protection for the child in the home of a German immigrant who nursed him "with more than a mother's care" and called a doctor. The German woman cared for her patient day and night.

When the child's mother finally found her boy, she knelt by his bed and prayed, thanking God for restoring her son to her. But her joy was short lived. The boy died a short time later. Simmons's mother and the baby survived the raid unhurt, but the house had been fired and lay in ruins.

During the riots, Shaw's father, who had founded the National

Freedmen's Relief Association, was a natural target for mob violence. It was rumored that his house would be burned, so Francis Shaw saw to it that his wife and daughters were spirited away to safety. Francis Shaw himself and his son-in-law George Curtis stayed on, on Staten Island, becoming part of an armed patrol protecting the neighborhood from an attack which, fortunately, never came.

With Hallowell and a handful of other officers, Shaw climbed one of Folly Island's sand hills where he could see the distant Federal vessels shelling Wagner. The rains had cleared the atmosphere. The sky was bright. A fresh breeze came up bringing the sounds of the incessant Federal cannonade. Beyond the gentle slopes of Morris Island, smoke hung over the naval vessels.

Brigadier General Talaiferro, who had served with distinction under Stonewall Jackson, commanded the Confederate forces on Morris Island. Talaiferro had ordered his soldiers at Fort Wagner to take cover during the bombardment. Most of his infantry soldiers and artillery men, excepting the gunners themselves, had been told to stay within the bombproof behind the southeast bastion of the fort. Talaiferro had sandbagged all but the few guns that provided sporadic replies to the Federal army's and navy's cannonade. Outside the body of the fort, two companies of the First South Carolina Battalion lay behind a ridge of sand called the "outer work." Inside the fort, the remainder of the South Carolina battalion, most of whom were natives of Charleston, and the battle-hardened Fifty-First North Carolina awaited the attack. The Confederates were bearing their ordeal bravely.

While Shaw and his men waited on Folly Island, the commanders of the various Federal brigades and correspondents from magazines and newspapers of the North began to gather on Morris Island's highest sand hill. Charleston, the objective of every soldier in the department, was just northwest beyond the low hills of James Island, its commanding spires, houses and public buildings outlined clearly against the sky. The hill afforded a fine view of the beautiful harbor. Attenuated clouds slashed the breadth of the azure sky. The water was blue in the distance and greener close by. On the far side of Sumter, the reflected sun sparkled on the surface of the main ship channel. The sandy islands and points of land across the water stood out sharply in the sun. Sumter itself could be clearly seen. The fort looked like a chunk of sculptured rock and its flag

snapped in the late morning breeze. A man with sharp eyes could
see the forts and batteries that ringed the harbor, most of them
ready to serve their guns in support of Wagner.

Fort Wagner, double-bastioned and built of palmetto log revet-
ments, mounting a liberal sprinkling of thirty-two pounders, a sea-
coast howitzer and an assortment of other guns, seemed now to be
losing its shape. Forty-one pieces of Federal artillery, captured guns
and the guns of the navy were finding their mark, kicking up sand
in and around the massive earthwork. To the men on the hills,
it seemed that the fort must be badly crippled. Indeed this was
one of the heaviest single bombardments of the Civil War, but
by the time it ended at four o'clock no gun would be crippled and
just a handful of men would be wounded or dead.

The brigade commanders gathered around Brigadier General
Truman Seymour, commanding the assault, and a discussion began.
Some brigade commanders protested that the assault would be
folly, but Seymour thought the attempt should be made. Colonel
H. S. Putnam, commanding a brigade, was a vociferous dissenter.
Putnam said, "I did not think we could take the fort so; but
Seymour overruled me. Seymour is a devil of a fellow for dash."

Putnam later remarked to an officer in his own regiment, the
Seventh New Hampshire, "We are going into Wagner like a flock
of sheep." Shaw's brigade commander, General Strong, unlike
Strong's classmate, Colonel Putnam, agreed with Seymour that the
fort could be taken by direct assault.

Late in the afternoon, the Fifty-Fourth was ferried across to Morris Island, landing on the shore where, a week before, the initial
attack had been launched in pine boats. Shaw and Adjutant James
rode forward to report to General Strong. Now the island was quiet,
the fort was silent, the Federal bombardment had ceased and, inside
the battered walls of the work, Talaiferro's gunners removed the
sandbags that protected the guns and wheeled the guns into position, making ready for the attack.

Strong told Shaw that they would storm the fort. He looked
straight at Shaw. "You may lead the column if you say yes. Your
men, I know, are worn out, but do as you choose."

Adjutant James remembered that Shaw's face brightened and
before he answered he turned to James and told him to go back
to the landing and tell Hallowell to bring up the regiment.

James found Hallowell and most of the men asleep on the beach. He woke Hallowell and gave him the order. The flags were unfurled and the regiment marched forward to Strong's headquarters.

Strong was a warmhearted man. He had won the affection of his officers and men by sharing their discomforts and risks. In the initial attack on Morris Island, he had exposed himself to great danger. Now he walked along the line with Shaw. He expressed surprise at finding the men in such excellent spirits. He stopped and talked to individual Negro soldiers saying he was sorry they had had so little rest. He told them he wished he could give them food and drink, but that time was short and they must move right up to the head of the column. Shaw sent the regiment forward with Hallowell and went with Strong to Strong's tent.

The correspondents, watching from the sand hills, were held spellbound by the scene below. The camps, nestling in the dunes, were deserted now; the countless blue-coated soldiers were gathering and forming—preparing to attack. The ground in front of the fort was scarred and pocked with great shell holes and the moat that ran along the base of the fort, fed by the waters of the sea, sloshed over into the nearest chasms. Just after six o'clock, the correspondents spotted a single regiment marching to the front along the middle road which ran north and south, just below them, seaward of their vantage point. At the head of the column were the regimental flags, curling gently as the evening breeze freshened. As the regiment marched, the advancing column drew a couple of ineffective shots. No one faltered or lost direction, but the standard bearers furled the flags so they wouldn't attract the enemy's fire. The men on the hills saw the commander of the color company face the flags as he walked, pointing to them with his sword, and at his command they were unfurled and fluttered free again.

About 6:30, Strong and Shaw rode toward the front. Strong was all spit and polish and a yellow bandana fluttered at his neck. Shaw wore light blue trousers and a staff officer's jacket with silver eagles on his shoulders. The horses picked their way forward through the low undergrowth for a short distance, then Shaw begged Strong's leave and turned back. He sought out his friend, Edward L. Pierce, acting as a correspondent for the *New York Daily Tribune*, whom he had seen at Strong's headquarters and who had visited Shaw on St. Helena. Shaw gave Pierce some of his

letters and personal papers, asking that they be sent to his family
if he was killed or captured in the coming assault. He shook Pierce's
hand, remounted and rode at a fast clip toward the front. He didn't
look for Strong but rode straight to his regiment to give instructions. The regiment was marched to the right, toward the sea and
halted close to the waves, the men on the right standing on the
hard-packed beach. Then Shaw dismounted and sent his horse back.

Hallowell asked Shaw if he would send the things that remained
in his pockets back to the rear and Shaw said, "No, they may as
well go with me."

Hallowell wrote later, "The regiment was formed in two lines;
the Colonel taking the right wing, which was in the front."

The men were ordered to lie down, their bayonets fixed, their
muskets loaded but not capped. While the officers waited for the
order to advance Shaw walked over to Hallowell and said, "Ned,
I shall go in advance of the men with the National Flag, you keep
the state flag with you. It will give the men something to rally
round. We shall take the fort or die there. Good bye! If I do not
come back, take my field glass." Then the two men parted. Hallowell remembered that Shaw was in good spirits. "He seemed happy
and cheerful, all of the sadness had left him and I am sure he
felt ready to meet his fate."

There were six hundred members of the Fifty-Fourth waiting for
the signal to attack. Some sickness, the necessity of leaving a large
camp guard on St. Helena and the losses sustained on James Island
had thinned the ranks. A fatigue detail of eighty men was on Morris Island but would not take part in the attack. Besides Shaw,
Hallowell and Adjutant James, nineteen of Shaw's officers waited
for the signal to attack. Surgeon Stone prepared to care for the
wounded. As was the custom, the band musicians were ordered
to act as stretcher-bearers.

As the sun plunged into the sea, a fresh breeze came up. The
sound of sporadic cannon fire mingled with the roll of distant
thunder. Once in a while, in a spell of quiet, the dash and hiss
of the waves could be heard. As the twilight deepened, a heavy
fog gathered over the sea. Men lay all around and as far to the
rear as the eye could pierce the gloom. Now and then an adjutant
rode by, looking up and down the lines.

There was very little nervousness in the ranks, but Shaw's soldiers had lost their usual lightheartedness. They were quiet now. A cannon ball passed over, close above the heads of the men. One man moved nervously. Hallowell spoke sharply, telling the man to be silent. Another said good-naturedly, "I guess the major[1] forgets what kind of balls them is!"

General Strong appeared, mounted as before on a great gray charger, Beside him rode two aides and two orderlies. Strong said, "Boys, I am a Massachusetts man, and I know you will fight for the honor of the State. I am sorry you must go into the fight tired and hungry, but the men in the fort are tired too. There are but three hundred[2] behind those walls and they have been fighting all day. Don't fire a musket on the way up, but go in and bayonet them at their guns."

Pointing to the man with the national flag, Strong asked, "If this man should fall, who will lift the flag and carry it on?"

Shaw was standing close to Strong. He took a cigar from between his teeth. "I will," he said.

His men cheered his pledge and Strong and his aides and orderlies rode off, the tails of their horses switching in the gloom. Silently the officers grasped each other's hands, then slid their revolvers around to the fronts of their jackets. Shaw walked quietly among his troops. There had always been a touch of austerity in his relations with his men. Now, one remembered, he spoke to them warmly, with evident affection. "I want you to prove yourselves," he told them. "The eyes of thousands will look on what you do tonight."

Shaw's manner was intent and watchful, but he seemed composed and moved easily. A fellow officer remembered that he was pale, that "a slight twitching at the corners of his mouth plainly showed that the whole cost was counted. . . ."

Shaw finished his tour. As darkness fell, there was sporadic fire from the Federal guns and, once in a while, a shot from the fort. One shell passed between the lines, another fell into the sea at the right. When it seemed that the waiting could be borne no longer, the signal to advance was passed. The time was 7:45. Shaw walked briskly along the line and stood in the center. He barely raised

---

[1] Hallowell was a Lieutenant Colonel at the time of the attack on Wagner but the men still called him "the major."

[2] General Strong was wrong. Emilio says that 1,700 manned the work.

his voice, but it was clearly heard. His men stood up. Shaw said, "Move in quick time until within a hundred yards of the fort, then double quick and charge!" He paused a moment, unsheathed his sword and issued a sharp command to march.

Shaw led the advance, walking steadily over the sand, his eyes straining into the dark. All was silent except for the scrape of boots against the sand. Once in a while a man whispered and a corporal or sergeant would motion him to silence. From the right came the sound of the sea as it enveloped the beach and was sucked back. As the way narrowed, commands were heard as the sergeants tried to straighten the lines. Into the funnel formed by swamp on the left and sea on the right, the regiment moved, its flags in front. The white banner of the state of Massachusetts could be seen by the soldiers in the rear, fluttering like a great bird in the night.

As Shaw advanced, the guns at Sumter and on Sullivan's and James Islands sought out the regiment, but the occasional shells fell wide or short. In spite of dwindling space, the lines were held. Now the men on the right had to march in the sea. They were ankle-deep as the waves slapped the sand and the water, as it spread up the beach, foamed and frothed around their knees. To Shaw, marching just above the wash of the waves, with his strong presentiments of death, this walk must have been a waking nightmare. The way grew narrower and the men on the flanks fell back. Shaw held his position in front of the center of the shrinking phalanx.

When the fort was just two hundred yards ahead, the enemy opened fire. As expected, there was raking fire as well as direct. All at once "a sheet of flame, followed by a running fire, like electric sparks, swept along the parapet."

The men remembered a succession of brilliant flashes. The murderous fire that poured from the fort had instant effect. Men were struck all around, spinning to the ground in a dance of death. Now the bludgeoned sand, rutted and pocked by Federal guns, was ploughed by Confederate shot and shell. "There had been no stop, pause or check at any period of the advance, nor was there now."

Shaw's sword flashed in the yellow light as he dashed forward, urging his men to the charge. His sword whipped the air, bringing on his charging men. The thud and boom of the flashing cannon seemed to split the brains of the oncoming men. The scene was lit by a pulsing, varicolored light. Shaw's men fell forward into the shell holes and clambered out, moving behind him across the now deserted outer work toward the moat and the rutted wall of the fort. The ground behind Shaw was a wasteland of dead and broken men. But more swept onward over the bodies of their fallen comrades. Now the southeast bastion loomed out of the dark like the blunt prow of a foundering ship. Shaw passed the bastion, running obliquely toward a point where four guns boomed in the dark. Hallowell remembered, "I saw him again, just for an instant, as he sprang into the ditch; his broken and shattered regiment were following him. . . ."

A private remembered seeing his Colonel approaching the massive sloping wall, his legs churning the salty waters, his body bent forward into the charge. Shaw was pale as snow, his mouth was set in a firm, hard line.

Now gunners appeared on the crest, depressing their pieces, firing down the angle of earth, straight into the faces of the advancing men. Shaw, wet to the waist, scrambled up the rampart, his voice ringing clear in a moment of silence, his bright sword pointing toward the stars. His men saw him etched black against the deep night sky, then caught in a flash of cannon fire. All at once he crumpled and pitched headlong into the fort.

18.

Captain Russel, the talkative nineteen-year-old officer from New York City, fell near the base of the fort and Captain Simkins, as he knelt to help him, was instantly struck—falling across Russel's lifeless body. Simkins never moved again.

Until Shaw was hit, not a shot was fired by any member of his regiment. The men who had followed him to the top of the fort engaged in hand-to-hand combat with their enemy. Fists, bayonets and rifle butts came into play, and the men of the Confederate garrison made free use of their gun-rammers and handspikes. Wounded and dead men fell back from their hold on the sandbagged ridge and pitched downward into the moat. Now, against the background of earth-shaking sound and the rattle of musket fire, came the crack of the pistols of Shaw's officers. Sergeant Major Lewis Douglass, elder son of the Negro leader, shouted in his bellowing voice, urging the stormers up the slope. Both of Douglass's boys were spared that night. Sergeant Carney, who had taken the national colors from the hands of the fallen color bearer, fought them to the top of the fort and set them beside the regimental colors which someone else had planted there.

After a spate of hand-to-hand fighting, some of the men who had clung to the top of the work began to fall back on the slope to avoid certain death where they stood outlined against the sky, an easy target for Southern marksmen. Here Shaw's men directed musket fire at the soldiers inside the fort. Hand grenades and lighted shells were thrown from inside the fort, killing some of the Negroes who clung to the slope. One wounded private lay on his back, a shattered arm hanging loosely by his side, and with his good hand piled cartridges on his chest to feed a rifle being brought into play by one of the officers who was taking a toll of Confederate gunners. One dashing Confederate, stripped to the waist, stood silhouetted against the sky, dealing out death with devastating accuracy until he was felled when three of Shaw's riflemen fired at him at once.

Now the officers and men on the slope must move forward to death or capture, or retreat through the hellish door by which they had come. Some moved forward but most, seeing that the attack had failed, retreated across the moat and took their chances crossing the moat and the rutted sand beyond. One wounded officer hid in the marsh near Vincent's Creek for several days until he was found by a Yankee picket, nearly starving, covered with sand and his own blood.

Desultory fighting was still going on. But it was clear now that the great charge which had hit the fort with all the impact that any regiment could have delivered, had long since spent its initial fury.

So fast was the advance of Shaw's regiment that it had been repulsed before the arrival of the following elements of Strong's brigade. Strong, always in the thick of the fighting himself, led the rest of his brigade into the mouths of the enemy's cannon. He hit the fort at the southeast bastion, and an action followed which was similar to that engaged in by Shaw. Here Strong was severely wounded and his attack met much the same fate as Shaw's.

When General Seymour, described by Putnam as "a devil of a fellow for dash," received reports that his leading brigade had not taken the fort, he ordered Putnam into the fray. Putnam proved he had plenty of dash himself. He led his brigade straight into the face of wicked enemy fire and, during the advance, was shot in the head. Putnam's One-Hundredth New York Regiment advanced and halted within musket range of the southeast bastion where, in the dark, they mistook their own men for enemy soldiers. Here they poured a volley or two into Putnam's New Hampshire Regiment and some of Shaw's men who had joined Putnam, and then retired—having unwittingly done the devil's work. Now Brigadier General Thomas Stevenson's brigade, designated as reserve and including Colonel James Montgomery's contraband regiment, moved forward but was soon sent back.

Ned Hallowell had been wounded in the groin before reaching the crest, and brave little Captain Emilio, slight of build and quick of mind, found himself commanding what was left of the regiment. He gathered the men around him in the dark and ranged them along an irregular trench and thin line of sand—the remains of the battered outer work. There he waited for a counterattack that never came.

The work of the One-Hundredth New York wasn't the only work of the devil done that night. Captain Emilio describes the final horror. "Upon the beach in front of the siege line, drunken soldiers of the regular artillery, with swords and pistol shots barred the passage of all to the rear. They would listen to no protestations that the regiments were driven back or broken up, and even brutally ordered wounded men to the front. After a time, their muddled senses came to them on seeing the host of arrivals, while the vigorous actions of a few determined officers who were prepared to enforce free passage, made further opposition perilous."

Brave Sergeant Carney, who had fought the national colors to the top of the work, now fought them back again. Carney was a religious boy, had lived for a time in Norfolk, Virginia, then moved to New Bedford, Massachusetts. He had done odd jobs for a living, trying to save enough money to enter the Christian ministry. He was one of the men recruited by James Grace, who, incidentally, would survive the war and go back to his family. In the end, when the fort lay silent, Carney would half-crawl, half-stagger into the field hospital that nestled in the dunes behind the lines. Bringing off the flag had cost him wounds in his chest and in his arms and legs. As he entered the lamplit tent with the flag in his hand, some of the wounded raised themselves from their straw beds and cheered the boy. Men who were there and survived that night say that Carney smiled and said that he had done no more than his duty— that the "dear old flag" had never touched the ground.[1]

The Confederates were jubilant that their great earthwork had proved impregnable. General Beauregard telegraphed General Joseph E. Johnston and several other Confederate colleagues,

PRAISE BE TO GOD. ANNIVERSARY OF BULL RUN GLORIOUSLY CELEBRATED.

Edward L. Pierce reported the scene as the fighting ended. "The battle is over; it is midnight; the ocean beach is crowded with the

---

[1] Sergeant Carney lived to take part in the ceremonies at the unveiling of the Shaw monument on Memorial Day in 1897.

dead, the dying and the wounded. It is with difficulty that you can urge your horse through to Lighthouse Inlet. Faint lights glimmer in the sand-holes and rifle pits where many a poor bleeding soldier has lain down to his last sleep."

The soft, warm light of Sunday's dawn illuminated a desolate scene. The dead sprawled on Wagner's slopes, and at the bottom of the moat they lay in a pile like a swarm of insects struck by a pestilence. Negroes and whites were strewn together along the white sands for three quarters of a mile, some washed by the waves whose eternal dirge sounded in the ears of the men who still lived. Behind the great mound of sandy earth, the sun touched the spires of Charleston whose citizens were opening their eyes and wondering what they would wear to church. And down on South Battery Street, early risers looked across the waters of the misty harbor with a feeling of pride in the mighty defenses that looked out to sea— keeping the ships of the Federal navy at bay and the Yankee hordes from overrunning their streets and pretty gardens.

A flag of truce was sent across to Wagner but it was refused, the Confederate Commander asserting that he had plenty of surgeons and medical supplies, and plenty of soldiers to bury Yankee dead. John T. Luck, an Assistant Surgeon of the United States Navy who was attached to the gunboat *Pawnee*, provided the only detailed report of what happened inside the fort that day. Luck was taken prisoner while caring for the wounded. When he entered the fort, he was shown the body of a United States colonel who lay where he had fallen, beside a powerfully built Negro sergeant. The fallen colonel must have been Shaw.

That afternoon, Surgeon Luck and the soldiers taken in the assault were moved by boat to Charleston and marched through the streets amid jeers and catcalls to the turreted jail on Magazine Street.

Luck wrote what he knew of the burial of those who had fallen. "All the officers killed in the assault were decently buried, excepting Colonel Shaw. His remains were thrown into a trench with those of his privates, and then covered up. I did not see this but was told by General Hagood, commanding Rebel forces at Morris Island, that such would be the case, and was afterward told by another Rebel officer that it had been done."

In another letter written by Luck which appeared in the *Army and Navy Journal,* General Hagood was held responsible for Shaw's burial. Luck asserted that Hagood had said, "I shall bury him in the common trench with the Negroes that fell with him." A less restrained utterance attributed to Hagood was repeated with bitterness throughout the North. "He is buried with his niggers." In New England the phrase was used in several verses written to the memory of Shaw by members of that company of literary warriors who grieved the death of a fallen son.

Confederate officer Lieutenant Iredell Jones wrote words of praise for Shaw and his men. "The negroes fought gallantly, and were headed by as brave a colonel as ever lived." Jones described Shaw's men as a fine-looking set of soldiers—"large, strong, muscular fellows."

Inspired by Shaw's sacrifice, Ralph Waldo Emerson set down lines that became familiar:

> So nigh is grandeur to our dust,
> So near is God to man,
> When duty whispers low, *Thou must,*
> The youth replies, I can.

On Staten Island, Shaw's parents rose to their hour of trial. When Shaw's father heard that efforts would be made to recover the body of his son, he wrote to General Gillmore asking that his son's remains lie where they were. The burial was fitting. Robert himself could have wanted no better. William Lloyd Garrison hailed Francis Shaw's decision, "Your letter to General Gillmore, concerning the removal of the body of Robert, thrilled my heart. . . ."

Letters of praise and sympathy flooded the Victorian house in West New Brighton. Young Henry James, troubled, as was his older brother William, at his passive role in the war, wrote, "I feel for you and Mrs. Shaw and the girls, more than I can put in fitting words. . . . It is a great leaf in God's book of life, now fully turned over for you, and I cannot but believe the lesson of it will be erelong altogether welcome. . . . In the mystical Creation, we are told that 'the evening and the morning were the first day'. . . . This is because in Divine order all progress is from dark to bright, from evil to good, from low to high, and never contrariwise." Morris Copeland wrote, "I saw the short telegraphic despatch, and as the awful fact stood clear before me, it seemed that God might have spared us this blow. . . ."

Sergeant Simmons, whose nephew had been killed in the riots in New York, was one of the soldiers who had been taken to Charleston. He and Sergeant Carney had been two of four men cited for exceptional gallantry in the recent action. Simmons had received a wound in the arm but hadn't been bothered by it at first. Now, as he languished in Charleston jail, it flared up and gave him so much pain that he was removed to the Old Marine Hospital whose windows overlooked the jailyard. Here the arm was amputated and here Simmons died.

About fifty men entered the hospital with Sergeant Simmons and, of these, perhaps thirty died. About one hundred of Shaw's men had been taken uninjured. Assistant Surgeon Luck wrote later that shortly after the Negro soldiers arrived in Charleston, "the Rebel government gave them to the State of South Carolina, that the State might make such disposition of them as it wished."

On August 10, 1863, Governor Bonham of South Carolina ordered the provost-marshal's court for the Charleston district convened for the trial of two of Shaw's soldiers. Their names are not on record but they were presumably among the few members of the Fifty-Fourth who had been slaves. Lincoln's proclamation of July 30 had had its effect.[2] The Confederates were leery of playing fast and loose with free Negroes from the North. Nelson Mitchell and Edward McCrady, eminent South Carolina attorneys, elected to defend the Negroes and, after hearing the arguments, the court ruled that it did not have jurisdiction over the men because they had not been South Carolina slaves. Governor Bonham was not pleased with the findings of the court but, because of pressure from Jefferson Davis and other quarters, he did not pursue the matter further.[3]

---

[2] Lincoln's proclamation (see p. 150) made Jefferson Davis reluctant to allow action to be taken against captured Negro soldiers. James A. Seddon, Davis's Secretary of War, wrote Bonham on September 1, 1863 that the whole question was "fraught with present difficulty and future danger." (See The War of the Rebellion . . . Official Records . . ., Series II, Vol. VII, pages 673, 703-4.)

[3] Governor Bonham might have been influenced by a letter from his cousin Sallie Butler, written at Greenville, S.C. on September 21, 1863. "I have been asked by a member of Campbell Williams' family to write and beg you to spare these negroes on *his* account. He is a prisoner in the hands of the Yankees, & has been selected to be *hung* in retaliation for those negroes which we have taken. This poor Mother has just lost a noble son in the battle of Brandy Station & now this son is to be hung. We heard

During the period of their trial, the men were imprisoned at Castle Pinkney on Shute's Folly Island in Charleston Harbor, just a stone's throw across the water from the complex of docks on the eastern edge of Charleston's peninsula. By the time Surgeon Luck left Charleston, the men had been taken back to the cheerless jail on Magazine Street where they lived in tattered tents in the open jailyard, under the shadow of a crudely constructed wooden gallows.

At the United States Army hospital in Beaufort, Edward Pierce, to whom Shaw had given his belongings when he turned back from his ride to the front with General Strong, wrote of the suffering of badly wounded officers and men who had been removed by steamer for intensive care. According to Pierce, General Strong was badly wounded though the nature of his wound was not set down. The attractive and youthful General asked first for Shaw, and, hearing that the Colonel had probably been killed, sent a message to his parents speaking of his love and respect for his fellow soldier. Before he died, Strong made a statement to Pierce about the conduct of the men of Shaw's regiment. "The Fifty-Fourth did well and nobly; only the fall of Colonel Shaw prevented them from entering the fort. They moved up as gallantly as any troops could, and with their enthusiasm they deserved a better fate."

Hallowell was luckier than Strong. When his wound had partially healed, he was sent home to Philadelphia where he recovered completely. During his convalescence, he was visited by Charlotte Forten and George L. Stearns. When he heard the news of the attack on Wagner, Stearns had written of the men, "I feel that they are my children whom I induced to rush into the jaws of death. Many of the names of the privates wounded are familiar to me and I can recall many of their faces. I should sometimes be tempted to say, 'Oh Lord how long?' did I not clearly see that this baptism of fire was necessary for the regeneration of both races."

After his visit to Hallowell in Philadelphia, Stearns wrote, "Ned Hallowell is doing finely; he was removed to the sofa yesterday for the first time. He is anxious to get back to the regiment."

the matter had been left entirely in your hands. . . . Mrs. Williams is a widow & in affliction at this time. He is so *young* and so dear to his family." (From the Milledge Luke Bonham Papers, South Caroliniana Library, University of South Carolina.)

Hallowell did return to his regiment. He served as its colonel until it was disbanded. The regiment would march again through the streets of Boston, hailed this time as conquering heroes. Hallowell, by then a brevet brigadier general, would call his officers around him[4] and thank them for long and faithful service.

When she heard that the hospital at Beaufort was filling with wounded, Charlotte Forten hurried over to Port Royal and did what she could for the suffering men. No testimony could have been more eloquent than hers. Two days after the attack on Wagner, she had written, "For nearly two weeks we have waited, oh how anxiously for news of our regiment which went, we know to Morris Island to take part in the attack on Charleston. To-night comes news, oh, so sad, so heart sickening. It is too terrible, too terrible to write. We can only hope it may not all be true. That our noble, beautiful young Colonel is killed, and the regiment cut to pieces! I cannot, cannot believe it. And yet I know it may be so. But oh, I am stunned, sick at heart."

In the following days, she worked with the surgeons and nurses in the wards of the hospital. Mrs. Rufus Saxton, wife of the popular Military Governor, asked her to mend the "pantaloons" and the jackets of the fallen men. "It was with a full heart that I sewed up bullet holes and bayonet cuts. Sometimes I found a jacket that told a sad tale—so torn to pieces that it was far past mending. After awhile I went through the wards. As I passed along I thought 'Many and low are the pallets, but each is the face of a friend.'"

Of one soldier, Charlotte Forten wrote, "Another Sergeant suffers great pain, being badly wounded in the leg. But he too lies perfectly patient and uncomplaining. He has such a good, honest face. It is pleasant to look at—although it is black. He is said to be one of the best and bravest men in the regiment."

Charlotte Forten was one of those who thought about Shaw's wife. "I know it was a glorious death. But oh, it is hard, very hard for the young wife, so late a bride."

Nine months later, when Negro enlistment in the Northern army had become commonplace, Mrs. Robert Gould Shaw watched New York's first Negro regiment march off to war. The people of the city, where a short time before Negroes had dangled from the

---

[4] Some officers were Negroes at the time the regiment was disbanded.

lampposts, gave its first Negro regiment a tumultuous send-off. Those who knew her were mightily moved at the sight of pretty little Mrs. Shaw whose husband's work had helped pave the way for the recruitment of the Twentieth Regiment United States Colored Troops.

Now the narrow neck of sand where Shaw was buried with his men is washed by Atlantic storms. St. Gaudens's monument to Shaw and his men marks a place where the Colonel and his regiment passed by on their way to war.

To New Englanders of his own time, Shaw, in his youthful Victorian innocence, seemed a kind of saint. In the last few months of his life, in his latter days and final hours, he had drawn on his forefathers' deep convictions and sense of duty and his own devotion to the cause which had rekindled the imaginations of New England's poets and scholars, preachers and teachers and practical men. In his last hours, Shaw had indeed caught fire and to those who had devoted their lives to the breaking of the back of the American shame, his death was an evening and a dawn.

AUTHOR'S NOTE

There is no evidence that the Negroes of the Fifty-Fourth were chosen to lead the attack on Fort Wagner because they were thought of as black cannon fodder. Shaw had asked that he and his officers and men be given an important trust. General Strong, whose decision it was to ask Shaw and his regiment to lead the column, had developed an affection for Shaw and was a kindred spirit.[1] Strong would not have sent Shaw and his men to almost certain death unless he thought that the objective might be gained. Strong, after all, was exceptionally brave and was mortally wounded in pressing the supporting attack. There is no reason to suspect that Strong's superiors, in planning the storming of the work, were influenced by the thought that black men might be sacrificed instead of whites.

Responsibility for the fate of the Fifty-Fourth must fall on the shoulders of General Gillmore, of whose master plan the attack on Wagner was part, and on those of General Seymour his commander in the field. Seymour's optimism led him to believe that the work would give way to frontal assault. At the same time, for some unknown reason, he was slow to order Putnam's supporting column into the attack. Federal intelligence was faulty, as it was throughout much of the Civil War and, in this first great modern war, fiascos were as plentiful as sparrows in a barnyard. The fact remains that Shaw's regiment did itself proud. The thousands whose eyes were on them that night were left in little doubt as to what might be expected of Negro soldiers.

One recently published popular account of the attack on Wagner suggests that Shaw might have been foolish. Shaw might be criticized for leading his men into battle when they were tired and had had so little food and water but the mettle of Shaw's men had been tested on James Island. He knew and loved them and they returned his affection. It would have been contrary to Shaw's temper, to the temper of any good soldier, and contrary to the wishes of most of his men if Shaw had refused Strong's offer on the grounds that they all could have done with a good night's rest.

There were 181 Confederate casualties in the attack on Wagner and 1515 on the Union side. Of the latter, the majority were white soldiers, a number of them of high rank. Shaw's regiment had not landed on Morris Island in full strength. As we have seen, there were six hundred

---

[1] General Strong had consulted with General Seymour and Seymour, having heard of the bravery of Shaw's regiment on James Island and believing that his men were as capable as any men in his command, agreed that they could lead the assault. In view of Shaw's letter to Strong urging that his men be put into battle, it was undoubtedly Strong who suggested that Shaw's regiment lead the attack.

present. Numbers had been reduced by illness, in the action on James Island and a large camp guard had been left on St. Helena.

Immediately after the attack on Wagner, Sumter and Wagner were put under siege. In this operation, Naval bombardment was combined with that of the Army. The siege was a success. A Federal bombardment, from August 17 to 23, reduced Fort Sumter to a state of impotence and the Federal blockade was further tightened. Morris Island was evacuated by the Confederates on September 6. Wagner yielded to the spade not the bayonet.

When Charleston was finally evacuated by Confederate troops, in the closing days of the war, elements of the Fifty-Fourth and Fifty-Fifth Regiments were among those who marched triumphant into the city.

As soon as the news reached Governor Andrew that men of the Fifty-Fourth were in enemy hands, Governor Andrew made it known to President Lincoln that prompt action was necessary to protect these men from the kind of treatment that they had been promised by the Confederate government. Two Sections were added to Francis Lieber's General Order 100, "Instructions for the Government of Armies of the United States in the Field." The first of these asserted that no individual soldier was responsible for warlike acts. The second reaffirmed the fact that the law of nations recognized no distinctions of color. This second section promised retaliation against Confederate prisoners for enslavement of Federal ones. The President issued the following proclamation to reenforce the latter act.

Executive Mansion, Washington, July 30, 1863.

It is the duty of every government to give protection to its citizens of whatever class, color, or condition, and especially to those who are duly organized as soldiers in the public service. The law of nations and the usages and customs of war, as carried on by civilized powers, permit no distinction as to color in the treatment of prisoners of war as public enemies. To sell or enslave any captured person on account of his color, and for no offence against the laws of war, is a relapse into barbarism and a crime against the civilization of the age. The Government of the United States will give the same protection to all its soldiers; and if the enemy shall sell or enslave any one because of his color, the offence shall be punished by retaliation upon the enemy's prisoners in our hands.

It is therefore ordered that for every soldier of the United States killed in violation of the laws of war, a Rebel soldier shall be executed, and for every one enslaved by the enemy or sold into slavery, a Rebel soldier shall be placed at hard labor on the public works, and continue at such labor until the other shall be released and receive the treatment due a prisoner of war.

ABRAHAM LINCOLN.

By order of the Secretary of War,
E. D. Townsend, Assistant Adjutant-General.

Lincoln's proclamation, as we have seen, was effective in keeping the Confederate government from taking legal action against free Negroes captured while in Federal service. It did not, however, prevent atrocities in the field. Witness the massacre of captured Negro troops at Fort Pillow in April 1864.

In April 1864, the Congress of the United States passed an order which declared its Negro soldiers equal to its white ones. Part of this act cited the determination of the men of the Fifty-Fourth Massachusetts Regiment to accept nothing less than what was due them. This act referred to the "good conduct, the distinguished proficiency in military discipline, the cheerful, enthusiastic, and persistent valour" of the regiment. It cited the contribution of the officers and men of the regiment to the justice which would now be sought for all United States Negroes under arms. "To their determination under every privation, to accept no position lower than that to which they were justly entitled, are to be attributed in large measure, this full recognition of the equality of colored soldiers, and the dimunition, if not the ultimate destruction, of the monstrous and unfounded prejudice against their race."

It should be noted that Shaw's family, in memory of their son, contributed large sums of money to the rebuilding of the town of Darien, Georgia.

Thirty-eight Negro regiments took part in the massive Union invasion of Virginia in the summer of 1864. Here and in other theatres of the war Negro soldiers were known as hard fighters. Seventeen were recipients of the Congressional Medal of Honor. About 180,000 Negroes served in the Union Army, almost 10 percent of the total force. In Lincoln's opinion, they tipped the balance in favor of the Union.

P. B.

NOTES ON SOURCES

Numbered footnotes in the text never refer to sources. Except where otherwise noted, Shaw's own words, his telegrams, etc. have been copied from privately printed volumes whose title pages bear the names of no compilers. Copies of these volumes may be found in the Rare Book Division of the New York Public Library and at the Houghton Library, Harvard University catalogued under the name Shaw, Robert Gould 1837–1863. The volumes containing Shaw's letters, etc. are LETTERS R.G.S. 1864, MEMORIAL R.G.S. 1864 and LETTERS R.G.S. 1876. The most useful of the MEMORIAL R.G.S. 1864 volumes is the one at the Houghton Library, Harvard University. This volume contains corrections by Shaw's mother in her own hand. MEMORIAL R.G.S. 1864 contains, not only Shaw's own words, but letters of condolence, excerpts from newspaper accounts of various events concerning him and his regiment, etc. References to this volume are found in Notes on Sources but I have not burdened the notes with references to the other two volumes which contain nothing but Shaw's own letters. In the latter volumes, the letters appear in chronological order.

All books, pamphlets and magazines from which quotes are taken are listed in the bibliography. Notes on manuscript materials are found only under Notes on Sources. Abbreviated reference is made to all sources listed in the bibliography. Example: Quint, pg. 63. Titles are used only where an author's name appears in the bibliography more than once.

FOREWORD

CHAPTER ONE

CHAPTER TWO

CHAPTER THREE

p. 10   Fanny Kemble's reference to her marriage: Letter to Shaw's mother, Sarah Blake (Sturgis) Shaw, from Frances Anne Kemble. Sarah Blake (Sturgis) Shaw papers, Houghton Library, Harvard University.

p. 10   Fanny Kemble's description of Sorrento: Kemble, *Further Records*, p. 302.

p. 10   Fredericka Bremer's description of Fanny Kemble: Armstrong, p. 302.

p. 10   Maria Lowell's description of Fanny Kemble: Armstrong, p. 302.

p. 10   Lydia Maria Child on Fanny Kemble: Lydia Maria Child to Sarah Blake (Sturgis) Shaw. Sarah Blake (Sturgis) Shaw papers, Houghton Library, Harvard University.

p. 10   Fanny Kemble in "a perfect agony of distress for the slaves": Frances Anne Kemble to Sarah Blake (Sturgis) Shaw. Sarah Blake (Sturgis) Shaw papers, Houghton Library, Harvard University.

p. 11   Fanny Kemble on visit to the infirmary: Kemble, *Journal of a Residence on a Georgia Plantation*, 1961 edition, p. 74.

pp. 12, 13   Microfilm editions of the *New York Daily Tribune* were directly consulted for all quotes appearing on these pages. The date lines appear on the page.

p. 14   Marion, Mississippi *Republican* as quoted in the *New York Daily Tribune*: Microfilm edition.

CHAPTER FOUR

Quoted material in this chapter is from Shaw's letters in the volume published in 1876. On p. 17, Shaw quotes his mother. Harvard class reports were also used.

CHAPTER FIVE

p. 24   Yancy quoted: Fite, pp. 301–329.
Especially useful in reconstructing the atmosphere of New York in 1860: Miller's *New York As It Is*. Drawings, lithographs and rail maps of the period were also useful.

CHAPTER SIX

p. 30   Victorian phrases: Swinton, pp. 33–34. "It was worth a life, that march. . . ."

pp. 31–32   Theodore Winthrop describes the march: Swinton, pp. 38–39.

p. 32   Theodore Winthrop describes arrival in Philadelphia: Swinton, footnote, p. 43.

p. 33   The "rugged mate" sees a flag in the sky: Swinton, p. 65.

pp. 34, 35   The *New York Daily Tribune* quoted: Swinton, p. 113.

p. 35   Provender piled under Capitol dome: Swinton, footnote, p. 130.

CHAPTER SEVEN

p. 40   Colonel Gordon's description of the breaking of camp: Gordon, *Brook Farm to Cedar Mountain*, p. 25.

pp. 42, 43   John A. Andrew, Ralph Waldo Emerson and Wendell Phillips praise John Brown: Drew pamphlet, pp. 79–110.

p. 45   Frederick Douglass quoted: Douglass, Frederick, p. 96.

p. 46   William James writes of Josephine Shaw and James Russell Lowell, Jr.: Greenslet, p. 289.

p. 47   Greely Curtis on his friendship with Shaw: Shaw, Robert Gould, *The Monument to Robert Gould Shaw*, p. 31.

CHAPTER EIGHT

pp. 50, 51   General Banks takes measures to curb intemperance: Quint, p. 63.

p. 54   A bandsman of the Second Regiment teases a resident of Forestville: Quint, p. 75.

p. 55   Act of Congress applying to fugitive slaves and laborers: Cited in Catton's *Terrible Swift Sword*, p. 203. Source: *Congressional Globe*, 37th Congress, 2d Session, part IV, appendix 14.

CHAPTER NINE

p. 61   McClellan's caution as exemplified by the removal of his wife's silver from Washington, D.C.: Esposito, p. 65.

p. 62   London *Times* quoted: In John A. Scott's introduction in 1961 edition of Kemble's *Journal of a Residence on a Georgia Plantation*, p. xlviii. See Kemble.

p. 63   Men's reaction to McClellan: Quint, p. 133.

p. 65   Harsh judgment of McClellan: Esposito, p. 69.

p. 66   Lord Mansfield quoted: Dumond, p. 5.

p. 66   Ralph Waldo Emerson on the Emancipation Proclamation: Commager, pp. 72–73.

p. 67   The London *Times* on Lincoln's Proclamation: Rhodes, in footnote on p. 344.

CHAPTER TEN

p. 71   Andrew's letter to Shaw: Shaw, Robert Gould, *Memorial R.G.S.*, pp. 4–5.

p. 72   William James on Shaw's reluctance to accept Governor Andrew's offer: Shaw, Robert Gould *The Monument to Robert Gould Shaw*, p. 78.

p. 73   Shaw's mother's letter to Andrew: Pearson, p. 77.

p. 73   Henry Higginson remembers Shaw: Higginson, Henry Lee, p. 85.

p. 73   Marching ditty: Redding, p. 15.

p. 74   Letter to Shaw from his mother on hearing the news that he would accept Andrew's offer: Privately owned.

p. 75   Charles Russell Lowell on Shaw as colonel of "the Governor's Negro regiment": Cornish, p. 107.

p. 76   Higginson remembers visit from Shaw and Morse: Shaw, Robert Gould *The Monument to Robert Gould Shaw*, p. 29.

p. 77   Superintendent of the Census Joseph Kennedy's estimate of number of Negroes available in Massachusetts: Cornish, p. 107.

p. 77   Notice in *Boston Journal*: Emilio's *Brave Black Regiment*, pp. 8–9.

p. 78   Andrew praises Norwood Hallowell in a letter to Shaw's father: *Ibid.*, p. 4.

p. 78   Simkins on use of Negro troops: *Ibid.*, p. 7.

p. 78   Edward L. Pierce paraphrased by Emilio: *Ibid.*, p. 13.

p. 79   Wendell Phillips speaks at Joy Street Church: *Ibid.*, pp. 13–14.

p. 79   Frederick Douglass speaks at Joy Street Church: *Ibid.*, p. 14.

p. 80   Lieutenant Grace openly insulted in New Bedford streets: *Ibid.*, p. 10.

p. 81   Shaw to Charley Morse on gayety in Boston, mentions Annie Haggerty: Letter from Readville, March 23, 1863. Shaw papers, Massachusetts Historical Society.

CHAPTER ELEVEN

p. 83   Shaw to Charley Morse on condition of camp at Readville: Letter from Readville, March 23, 1863. *Ibid.*

p. 83   Shaw to Charley Morse about recruits from New Bedford: March 4, 1863. *Ibid.*

pp. 83, 84   Emilio and Surgeon General Dale comment on general character of Negro recruits: Emilio's *Brave Black Regiment*, pp. 19–21.

p. 84   Conversation between Andrew and Stearns as remembered by Nathan Haskell Dole in a letter to the *Boston*

Evening Transcript. See microfilm edition, May 22, 1897.

pp. 84, 85   Stearns describes the rigors of recruiting: Dole quotes Stearns's own words as Stearns wrote them for the Brooks-Usher *History of Medford*: *Ibid.*

p. 85   The *National Intelligencer* of March 16, 1863, pokes fun at Governor Andrew: cited in Cornish, p. 108.

p. 86   Shaw to Amos A. Lawrence: Letter from Readville, March 25, 1863. Lawrence papers at Massachusetts Historical Society.

p. 87   "Old Quin" quoted: *Dictionary of American Biography*, Vol. XV, Charles Scribner's Sons, New York, 1935.

p. 88   Exuberant telegram, Stearns to Andrew: quoted by Dole in the *Boston Evening Transcript*, May 22, 1897. See microfilm edition.

CHAPTER TWELVE

p. 91   Surgeon General Dale reports that Shaw's men were "gentlemen as well as soldiers": Emilio's *Brave Black Regiment*, p. 22.

p. 92   *Springfield Republican* quoted: Shaw, Robert Gould, Memorial R.G.S., 1863.

p. 92   Telegram from Stanton to Andrew: Quoted by Shaw in letter dated May 18, 1863, Shaw, Robert Gould, *Memorial R.G.S.*, 1863, p. 80.

p. 93   Dr. Bowditch raises a cheer for Shaw: Lader, p. 284. Source: Bowditch, Henry I. "Memorials of our Martyr Soldiers." Manuscript at Massachusetts Historical Society.

pp. 93, 94   Ellen Shaw quoted: Insert in a copy of McKay's *When the Tide Turned in the Civil War*. The Rare Book Division, Boston Public Library.

CHAPTER THIRTEEN

p. 94   John Greenleaf Whittier on the march of the Fifty-Fourth through Boston: McKay, p. 13.

p. 98   General Hunter's "Emancipation Proclamation": Quoted in Cornish, p. 35.

p. 98   Orders of War Department to Hunter's predecessor, Thomas W. Sherman: Cornish, pp. 33–34.

p. 99   Hunter on appearance of Shaw's men: Emilio's *Brave Black Regiment*, pp. 36–37.

p. 100   Thomas Wentworth Higginson remembers Shaw's "quiet power": Shaw, Robert Gould, *Memorial R.G.S.*, p. 151.

pp. 100, 101   Thomas Wentworth Higginson in *Army Life in a Black Regiment*, Higginson, T. W., p. 176.

CHAPTER FOURTEEN

CHAPTER FIFTEEN

CHAPTER SIXTEEN

p. 126   Emilio remembers young Confederate brought in dead: Emilio's *Brave Black Regiment*, p. 62.

p. 126   General Terry praises Shaw's regiment: *Ibid.*, p. 62.

p. 126   *The Reflector* quoted on the gratitude of the men of the Tenth Connecticut: *Ibid.*, p. 60.

p. 126   Ned Hallowell remembers Shaw's presentiments of death: Shaw, Robert Gould *Memorial R.G.S.*, p. 165.

CHAPTER SEVENTEEN

p. 130   Hallowell quotes himself and Shaw and remembers Shaw's state of mind on the morning of his final day: *Ibid.*, pp. 165–166.

p. 130   Simmons's letter: *Ibid.*, pp. 45–46.

p. 131   The account of the tragedy in Simmons's family during the Draft Riots: *Report of the Committee of Merchants for the Relief of Colored People Suffering from the Late Riots*, paraphrased and quoted.

p. 133   Union officers on Morris Island discuss assault, Colonel H. S. Putnam quoted: Emilio's pamphlet, *The Assault on Fort Wagner*, p. 6.

p. 133   General Strong asks Shaw if he will lead the column: Emilio's *Brave Black Regiment*, p. 72.

p. 135   Hallowell letter quoting Shaw and describing formation: Shaw, Robert Gould, *Memorial R.G.S.*, p. 166.

p. 135   Hallowell quotes Shaw, "Ned, I shall go etc." *Ibid.*, p. 166.

p. 136   "I guess the major forgets etc." Emilio's *Brave Black Regiment*, p. 76.

p. 136   Strong talks to Shaw's men, asks, "who will lift the flag and carry it on?", Shaw answers: *Ibid.*, p. 77.

p. 136   Shaw talks to men with evident affection: Ibid, p. 78.

p. 136   Emilio remembers Shaw's pallor: *Ibid.*, p. 78.

p. 137   Shaw's final instructions to his men, the order to charge. *Ibid.*, p. 79.

p. 137   Emilio remembers the enemy opening fire and, in the following paragraph, the steady advance of the Fifty-Fourth: *Ibid.*, p. 80.

p. 138   Hallowell describes Shaw's last moments: Shaw, Robert Gould *Memorial R.G.S.*, p. 166.

CHAPTER EIGHTEEN

p. 141   Beauregard's telegram quoted: Quarles, p. 17.

pp. 141, 142   Edward L. Pierce in the *New York Daily Tribune*. *Ibid.*, p. 17.

p. 142   Assistant Surgeon Luck on burial of Shaw: Shaw, Robert Gould *Memorial R.G.S.*, p. 180.

p. 143   Luck in the *Army and Navy Journal*: Emilio's *Brave Black Regiment*, p. 99.

p. 143   Confederate Lieutenant Iredell Jones praises Shaw and his men: *Ibid.*, p. 95.

p. 143   Garrison's letter to Shaw's father: Shaw, Robert Gould *Memorial R.G.S.*, p. 130.

p. 143   Henry James's letter to Shaw's father: *Ibid.*, p. 131.

p. 143   Morris Copeland reacts to the news of Shaw's death: *Ibid.*, p. 125.

p. 144   Surgeon Luck on disposition of Negro prisoners: *Ibid.*, p. 180.

p. 145   General Strong praises Shaw and his regiment: Emilio's *Brave Black Regiment*, p. 94.

p. 145   George L. Stearns on his feelings when he heard the news of the attack on Fort Wagner and his visit to Hallowell: Nathan Haskell Dole quotes Strong's own words as he wrote them for the Brooks-Usher *History of Medford*. See microfilm edition of the *Boston Evening Transcript*, May 22, 1897.

p. 146   Charlotte Forten in her diary on the fate of Shaw and his regiment: Forten, pp. 193, 194.

p. 146   Charlotte Forten mends uniforms: Forten, 194.

p. 146   She writes of a wounded sergeant: *Ibid.*, p. 195.

p. 146   She thinks of Shaw's wife: *Ibid.*, p. 196.

BIBLIOGRAPHY

BOOKS

Armstrong, Margaret, *Fanny Kemble, A Passionate Victorian*, New York: Macmillan & Co., 1938.

Botume, Elizabeth Hyde, *First Days among the Contrabands*, New York: Lee and Shephard 1893.

Bowen, James L., *Massachusetts in the War, 1861–1865*, Springfield: Clark W. Bryan, 1889.

Brooks, Van Wyck, *The Flowering of New England*, New York: E. P. Dutton & Co., Inc., 1957.

Browne, A. G., Jr., *Sketch of the Official Life of Governor Andrew*, New York: Hurd and Houghton, 1868.

Catton, Bruce, *The Coming Fury*, Garden City: Doubleday & Co., Inc., 1961.

———, *Terrible Swift Sword*, Garden City: Doubleday & Co., Inc., 1963.

Child, Lydia Maria, *Letters of Lydia Maria Child* (with an introduction by John Greenleaf Whittier), Boston: Houghton Mifflin Co., 1882.

Commager, Henry Steele, *The Great Proclamation*, New York: Bobbs Merrill Co., Inc., 1960.

Cornish, Dudley Taylor, *The Sable Arm*, New York: Longmans Green & Co., 1956.

Douglass, Frederick, *The Life and Writings of Frederick Douglass, III*, New York: International Publishers Co., Inc., 1952.

Dumond, Dwight Lowell, *Antislavery, the Crusade for Freedom in America*, Ann Arbor: The University of Michigan Press, 1961.

Emilio, Luis F., *A Brave Black Regiment, History of the Fifty-Fourth Regiment of Massachusetts Volunteer Infantry*, Boston: The Boston Book Co., 1891.

Esposito, Col. Vincent J. (ed.), *The West Point Atlas of the Civil War*, New York: Frederick A. Praeger, Inc., 1962.

Fite, Emerson David, *The Presidential Campaign of 1860*, New York: The Macmillan Co., 1911.

Forten, Charlotte, *The Journal of Charlotte Forten*, New York: Dryden Press, 1953.

Gordon, George H., *Brook Farm to Cedar Mountain in the War of the Rebellion*, Boston: James R. Osgood & Co., 1883.

———, *History of the Second Massachusetts Regiment of Infantry*, Boston: Alfred Mudge & Son, 1875.

Greenslet, Ferris, *The Lowells and Their Seven Worlds*, Boston: Houghton Mifflin Co., 1946.

Higginson, Henry Lee, Four Addresses (including one entitled "Robert Gould Shaw"), Boston: The Merrymount Press, 1902.

Higginson, T. W., *Army Life in a Black Regiment* (introduction by Howard Mumford Jones), East Lansing: Michigan State University Press, 1960.

Jones, Katharine M., *Port Royal Under Six Flags,* New York: Bobbs Merrill Co., Inc., 1960.

Keller, Allan, *Thunder at Harper's Ferry,* Englewood: Prentice-Hall Inc., 1958.

Kemble, Frances Anne, *Further Records 1848–1883,* New York: Henry Holt & Co., Inc., 1891.

———, *Journal of a Residence on a Georgia Plantation in 1838–1839,* New York: Harper & Bros., 1863.

———, *Journal of a Residence on a Georgia Plantation in 1838–1839* (edited by and with an introduction by John A. Scott), London: Jonathan Cape Co., Ltd., 1961.

Knox, Dudley W., *A History of the United States Navy,* New York: G. P. Putnam's Sons, 1948.

Lader, Lawrence, *The Bold Brahmins,* New York: E. P. Dutton & Co., Inc., 1961.

Leng, Charles W., *Staten Island and Its People,* I, New York: Lewis Historical Publishing Company, 1930.

Malin, James C., *John Brown and the Legend of Fifty-Six,* Philadelphia: The American Philosophical Society, 1942.

McKay, Martha Nicholson, *When the Tide Turned in the Civil War,* Indianapolis: The Hollenbeck Press, 1929.

Miller, James, *Miller's New York as It Is* or *Stranger's Guide Book,* New York: James Miller, 1860.

Nevins, Allan, *American Press Opinion, Washington to Coolidge,* Boston: D. C. Heath & Co., 1928.

Pearson, Henry Greenleaf, *The Life of John A. Andrew,* Boston: Houghton Mifflin Co., 1900.

Quarles, Benjamin, *Frederick Douglass,* New York: The Associated Press Publishers, 1948.

———, *The Negro in the Civil War,* Boston: Little Brown & Co., 1953.

Quint, Alonzo Hall (Chaplain), *Record of the Second Massachusetts Infantry,* Boston: James P. Walker, 1867.

Redding, Saunders, *The Lonesome Road,* Garden City: Doubleday & Co., Inc., 1958.

Rhodes, James Ford, *History of the United States from the Compromise of 1850,* IV, 1862–1864, New York: The Macmillan Co., 1902.

Scott, John Anthony, *Living Documents in American History,* New York: Washington Square Press, 1964.

Scott, Robert N., *The War of the Rebellion: A Compilation of the Official Records of the Union and Confederate Armies.* Series I, Vol. XXVIII, Part I, Washington: Government Printing Office, 1890.

Shaw, Robert Gould, *Letters,* Cambridge: Cambridge University Press, 1864.
——, *Letters,* New York: Collins & Brother, 1876.
——, *Memorial,* Cambridge: Cambridge University Press, 1864.
——, *The Monument to Robert Gould Shaw: Its Inception, Completion and Unveiling,* Boston & New York: Houghton Mifflin Co., 1897.
[The last two titles are normally listed under Shaw's name in library catalogs.]
Shaw, Major Samuel, *The Journals of Major Samuel Shaw* (with a life of the author by Josiah Quincy), Boston: Wm. Crosby & H. P. Nichols, 1847.
Sutherland, George C., *The Negro in the Late War,* Milwaukee: Burdick, Armitage & Allen, 1888.
Swinton, William, *History of the Seventh Regiment National Guard, State of New York, During the War of the Rebellion,* New York: Charles T. Dillingham, 1886.
Walkley, Stephen, *History of the Seventh Connecticut Volunteer Infantry:* Privately printed, circa 1905.
Werstein, Irving, *July* 1863 (author's note and bibliography only), New York: Julian Messner, 1957.
Wiley, Bell Irvin, *Southern Negroes,* New Haven: The Yale University Press, 1938.
Williams, George W., *History of the Negro Troops in the War of the Rebellion,* New York: Harper & Bros., 1888.

OFFICIAL RECORDS

The War of the Rebellion: A Compilation of the Official Records of the Union and Confederate Armies. Series I, Vol. XXVIII, Part I, Washington: Government Printing Office, 1890.

MAGAZINE ARTICLES

Coulter, E. Merion, "Robert Gould Shaw and the Burning of Darien, Georgia," *A Quarterly Journal of Studies in Civil War History,* Vol. 5, No. 5, State University of Iowa, December, 1959.
Forten, Charlotte, "Life on the Sea Islands," *The Atlantic Monthly,* XIII, May–June, 1864.
Higginson, T. W. et al., "The Shaw Memorial and the Sculptor St. Gaudens" (especially III: Colored Troops Under Fire by T. W. Higginson), *The Century Illustrated Magazine,* XXXII, May–October, 1897.
MacMaster, Richard K., "He Cast His Lot with Negro Troops," *New York State and the Civil War,* September–October, 1962.
Shaw, Robert Gould, "Letters," *Magazine of History,* Vols. 18 & 19, 1914.

PAMPHLETS

Boker, George H., *General Banks on the Bravery of Negro Troops,* Philadelphia: publisher unknown, circa 1863.

Drew, Thomas (comp.), *The John Brown Invasion,* Boston: J. Campbell, 1860.

Emilio, Luis F., *The Assault on Fort Wagner,* Boston: Rand Avery, 1887.

Teamoh, Robert T., *Sketch of the Life and Death of Colonel Robert Gould Shaw,* Boston: Privately Printed, 1904.

Whitehill, Walter Muir, *Boston and the Civil War,* Boston: Boston Athenaeum, 1963.

Report of the Committee of Merchants for the Relief of Colored People Suffering from the Late Riots, New York: G. A. Whitehorn, 1863.

In addition to works listed above, use was made of manuscript materials in the Massachusetts Historical Society, The Houghton Library, Harvard University and the Library of Congress. Quotes from two of these sources are listed in Notes on Sources. At the Massachusetts Historical Society, the papers of Robert Gould Shaw, 1837–1863, consisting mostly of letters written by Shaw to Charles Morse and documents relating to Shaw's military service as well as the Amos A. Lawrence papers were of special interest. The papers of Shaw's mother, Sarah Blake (Sturgis) Shaw at The Houghton Library were also useful.

Information was gathered in conversation with one of Robert Gould Shaw's collateral descendants. A few privately owned letters were in her possession, and one of these is quoted and so listed. The collateral descendant prefers to remain anonymous.

One by one the sea islands are becoming resorts though St. Helena and some of the others retain their natural character. The jail in Charleston still stands though it no longer houses prisoners. The Church of the Ascension in New York where Shaw and Annie Haggerty were married is still standing. Its cornerstone was laid in 1840 and extensive alterations were made on the interior in 1885. The present Fifth Avenue Hotel is not on the site where it was in Shaw's time. The house at 44 Beacon St. still stands and is, almost without question, as it was when Shaw lived there and when he and his regiment marched by. The Somerset Club, on Somerset Street when Shaw and the regiment passed by, now occupies quarters on Beacon Street.

INDEX